Communication, Language and Literacy

Irene Yates

 Brilliant Publications

Publisher's information

Brilliant Publications
1 Church View
Sparrow Hall Farm
Edlesborough
Dunstable, Bedfordshire
LU6 2ES

Tel: **01525 229720**
Fax: **01525 229725**
e-mail: **sales@brilliantpublications.co.uk**
Website: **www.brilliantpublications.co.uk**

Communication, Language and Literacy by Irene Yates
Illustrated by Charlie-Anne Turner

© Irene Yates 2003.

ISBN 1 897675 968

First published in the UK in 2003.
10 9 8 7 6 5 4 3 2 1

Printed in Malta by Interprint Ltd.

The right of Irene Yates to be identified as the author of this work has been asserted by her in accordance with the Copyright, Design and Patents Act 1988.

There are six books in the Foundation Blocks series, one for each of the key areas. Each book contains clearly laid-out pages, giving a wealth of activities, ideas and suggestions. For further details on how these books are structured and how they make implementing the QCA's Curriculum Guidance for the Foundation Stage easy, please see *Introduction* on page 6.

Other books in the Foundation Blocks series include:

Communication, Language and Literacy
by Irene Yates
Encourage children to develop good communication skills, extend their vocabulary, use language to help thinking, begin to link sounds and letters, use and enjoy books and start to develop writing skills.

Creative Development *by Mavis Brown*
Encourage children to explore the different art media and materials available, to recognize and explore sounds, to use their imagination, to express and communicate their ideas, thoughts and feelings using dance, movement, art, music and imaginary play or role play.

Mathematical Development
by Rebecca Taylor
The activities in this book will help children to use numbers, count to 10, recognize numerals to 9, begin to do simple calculations, and start to develop an understanding of shape, space and measurement.

Personal, Social and Emotional Development
by Mavis Brown
Help children to develop positive attitudes, self-confidence and high self-esteem. Encourage them to form good relationships with peers and adults; to understand what is right, what is wrong and why; and to develop self-care skills with a sense of community.

Physical Development
by Maureen Warner
Encourage children to move with confidence, control and co-ordination, using a variety of equipment. Help them to gain awareness of space, of themselves and of others and to recognize the importance of keeping healthy.

Please note that in **Links to home** we refer to the child's legal representative guardian/carer as 'parent'.

Communication, Language and Literacy

© Irene Yates
www.brilliantpublications.co.uk

Contents

Contents

© Irene Yates
www.brilliantpublications.co.uk

Introduction

- This book has over 145 differentiated activities set in real-life contexts relevant to pre-school children (3 to 5 years old). The activities aim to develop children's language skills in accordance with the *Curriculum Guidance for the Foundation Stage* (QCA 2000).

- All of the ideas, activities and tasks are designed to nurture and future language skills.

- There are four strands to language development:

    - Listening   (receptive)
    - Speaking   (active)
    - Reading   (receptive)
    - Writing   (active)

- All of these skills interact together and they are constantly developing throughout the whole or our lives. It is easy to see *why*, because they are skills. They are, simply, something we learn to *do* – not something we learn to *know*.

- Skills can only be learned in one way – through practice. They cannot be taught or learned in the same way that information is taught or learned. They are something that we have to keep trying at, failing at, trying again, succeeding, getting better.

- It is crucial that children are given lots of opportunities to extend their listening skills. This means listening to adults in relatively informal situations (story time, etc) and listening to their peers in relatively formal situations (circle time), as well as listening to both adults and peers in total informal situations – playing, following instructions, chatting, etc. When they are listening, they are always using the skills they have for thinking and understanding.

- Thinking and understanding skills are always ahead of speaking skills. Often, foundation stage children are afraid to put their thinking into words for fear of being 'wrong' or of being laughed at. Try to engender an attitude amongst all of your group where the children feel easy about speaking out loud even if they fear making 'mistakes'. There can be no such thing as 'failure' in terms of language skills, because the stage a child is at is the stage a child is at. Help children who are attempting to say new words – there is a belief that once you have used a word five times in an appropriate context, then that word belongs to you. In other words, you have made it a part of your *active vocabulary.* Active vocabulary is the language that you use as a matter of course in your thinking, speaking and writing.

- Skills cannot be developed in isolation. They are always being developed with *concepts* and *attitudes*. That is – we cannot develop the skills of listening unless we are listening about *something* (some concept). We cannot develop the skills of writing unless we are writing about *something* (some concept).

- All the time we are developing these skills we are learning and applying some *attitude* towards what we are doing. This is why it is so important that the children learn good attitudes towards what they are doing in their early formative years.

The things that they do, therefore, need to be fun, interesting and challenging enough to give them lots of confidence. Hopefully, it they enjoy reading and writing in the early stages they will have formed an attitude for life.

- Because language is concerned with the development of skills you will find that most of the activities in this book can be hooked on to any topic or project that you are exploring in your group. The tasks are designed to let you choose your own directions and to allow the children (and yourself) lots of exploration so that you can be sure that whatever you are doing has a sound developmental basis.

- The activities are divided into chapters merely to give you a useful tool to decide how to make up a consistently varied programme so that you are not, for example, doing 'reading activities' or 'speaking activities' all the time, but are giving the children plenty of encouragement and experience across the four strands.

- When you are teaching children the early stages of reading and writing, allow them to take the lead. The 'apprenticeship' approach is the best way forward, where you act as a role model and the children pick up their skills from you. For example, if you are following the words with your finger, from left to right, the children will learn that they are expected to read from left to right; if you are thinking about the first sound of a word, aloud, then the children will earn that this is how they will begin to write it.

- You need to stay aware that auditory and visual discrimination does not develop in all children at the same rate and this can greatly affect their language skills and abilities. Some children in the foundation stage may still have fuzzy hearing which will not let them discriminate different sounds particularly well, or they may not have the ability to perceive the differences between shapes of letters even though they can 'see' them properly. Don't take this as evidence that they are 'behind' the other children in their skills, rather that their physical maturation needs time to catch up. Practice, practice, practice is the key to helping them.

- To avoid the clumsy 'he/she' the child is referred to throughout as 'she'.

Communication, Language and Literacy

Planning

Where relevant the activities have been linked to sixteen topics commonly used in early years and primary settings. These are:

- Animals
- Celebrations
- Colours
- Families
- Food and shopping
- Gardening
- Health
- Homes

- Myself
- People who help us
- Seasons
- Shapes
- Toys
- Travel and transport
- Water
- Weather

- The topic appears in a shaded box at the top of each page. The other books in this series also use these same topics. While we have suggested topics, they are not set in concrete. All the activities can easily by modified to fit into a topic of your choice. The majority of activities in this book can be used with any topic.

- All activities are designed with the full curriculum in mind. Therefore they will all tie into other areas of the curriculum, giving you lots of opportunities for exploring Knowledge and Understanding of the World, Personal, Social and Emotional Development, Creative Development, Physical Development and Mathematical Development.

- Prior knowledge is not expected for any of the activities as the practitioner should choose an activity with the developmental stage of the child in mind.

- Although plenary sessions have not been included, it is taken as read that the practitioner would do lots of 'reviewing' activities, to give the children opportunities to verbalize what they have been doing, how they felt about it, and what they think they have achieved. It goes without saying that, hopefully, the practitioner would also take as many opportunities as possible to discuss with parents how they can build upon the experiences that the children have shared.

Logos used on the activity sheets

Box 1 – group size

This box indicates the number of children recommended for the activity, keeping safety and level of difficulty in mind. Less able children can achieve more difficult tasks with a smaller child to adult ratio. The group size indicates the size of group for the activity itself, rather than for any introductory or plenary sessions.

Box 2 – level of difficulty

This box uses a scale between 1 and 5 to depict the level of difficulty the task might present to the children. 1 indicates an activity suitable for children working in the yellow band of the Curriculum Guidance for the Foundation Stage; 5 indicates an activity suitable for able children in the reception class who are meeting the Early Learning Goals. As most settings have mixed age groups, the majority of the activities have been classified as easy so that the whole class can be involved. Higher levels can be achieved through outcome and the suggested extension activities.

Box 3 – time needed to complete the activity

The suggested time slots are only a guideline. Children need time to practise their skills, test their ideas and reflect upon their findings. Some children will wish to extend the original activity to pursue their own enquiries or improve upon their experiment.

Safety

Where relevant, additional safety notes are included on the sheets. You are advised to read these before commencing the activity.

Links to home

● The word 'parent' is used to refer to all those persons responsible for the child, and include mothers, fathers, legal guardians and primary carers of children in public care. The 'Links to home' suggest ways in which parents can continue and reinforce the learning that is experienced at the setting.

● Parents can give important information about their children and the child's experiences, on which the practitioner can build. It is essential that the practitioner finds out about any health problems, in particular any allergies.

● Parents can be a valuable resource, giving support when extra help is needed during visits out of the setting, and with more complex activities during designing and making. They can become the knowledgeable visitor, bringing their own language, culture and experiences to the setting.

● Parents are also a useful source of recycled materials, which are required for many of the tasks.

Safety

● Children are active learners, and investigative, exploratory and construction activities invariably involve the use of potentially dangerous equipment. Part of the learning process involves offering the child the opportunity to learn to use this equipment safely. As young children cannot anticipate danger, practitioners have to be vigilant and take part in a regular risk assessment exercise relevant to their own setting.

● Any rules issued by your employer or LEA should be adhered to in priority to the recommendations in this book; therefore check your employer's and LEA's Health and Safety guidelines and their policies on the use of equipment.

Templates and other resources

● On pages 171–179 you will find photocopiable templates to be used in conjunction with the relevant activity. The pieces will last much longer if they are either laminated or covered with sticky-back plastic.

● Also included are the words to many traditional rhymes (pages 180–186) and story lines to some traditional tales (pages 187–191).

© Irene Yates
www.brilliantpublications.co.uk

Assessment sheets

Assessment

- Each activity has learning objectives which are linked to the Knowledge and Understanding of the World curriculum.

- To assist the practitioner in the task of planning a balanced programme of experiences, the charts on the following pages show which activities address which of the QCA 'Stepping Stones'. The charts will also be useful for short-term planning, identifying future learning priorities and ascertaining whether support is required to achieve a level. The comments column can be used to record comments on the group as a whole, or for individual children. These sheets may be photocopied.

- Other evidence of the child's achievements in the form of (dated) early writing, dictations, drawings, paintings and photographs of 3D work can be kept in a portfolio. This album can also be a source of celebration and pleasure to look at in the future for the child and parent.

- These records should be retained for inspection.

Curriculum Guidance levels: | Yellow | | Blue | | Green | | E.L.G. | (Early learning group)

Stepping stone	Activities which address stepping stones	Comments
Use action, sometimes with limited talk that is largely concerned with the 'here and now'	Little Miss Muffit, Hey diddle diddle, Huff Puff, What can we do?	
Talk activities through, reflecting on and modifying what they are doing	Make and Play, Build a Den	
Use talk to give new meanings to objects and actions, treating them as symbols for other things	What does this do? Making Jigsaws	
Use talk to connect to ideas, explain what is happening and anticipate what might happen next	Set up a Fish 'n' chip shop, Transport	
Use talk, actions and objects to recall and relive past experiences	Wild Animal Park, Hospital Corner, Build a Castle	
Begin to use talk instead of action to rehearse, reorder and reflect on past experience, linking significant events from own experience and from stories, paying attention to sequence and how events lead into one another	Dressing up Box, Who shall I be?	

Stepping stone	Activities which address stepping stones	Comments
Begin to make patterns in their experience through linking cause and effect, sequencing, ordering and grouping	Build a Den, What's under here?	
Begin to use talk to pretend imaginary situations	Be a Pirate, Make a Call	
Use language to imagine and create roles and experiences	Be a Pirate, Acting Stones	
Use talk to organize, sequence and clarify thinking, ideas, feelings and events	Acting Stones, Space Shuttle	
Use words and/or gestures, including body language such as eye contact and facial expression to communicate	Making Jigsaws, What's under here?	
Use simple statements and questions often linked to gesture	Tell us about..., How do I feel?	
Use intonation, rhythm and phrasing to make their meaning clear to others	Make a Call, Fish and Chips, What's Outside?	
Have emerging self-confidence to speak to others about wants and interests	Tell us about..., How would I feel?	
Use simple grammatical structures	Make a Call, Where can Bear go?	
Ask simple questions often in the form of 'where' or 'what'	Make a Call, Collecting	
Talk alongside others, rather than with them. Use talk to gain attention and initiate changes. Use action rather than talk to demonstrate or explain to others	Collecting, What does it do?	
Initiate conversation, attend to and take account of what others say, and use talk to resolve disagreements	What is it?, What's Outside	
Interact with others, negotiating plans and activities and taking turns in conversation	Pass the Toy, Make and Play	
Listen to favourite nursery rhymes, stories and songs. Join in with repeated refrains, anticipating key events and important phrases	I Hear This, Taking Turns	
Respond to simple instructions	What's This?, Guess What it is?, Silly Words	

Communication, Language and Literacy

Stepping stone	Activities which address stepping stones	Comments
Listen to others in small one-to-one/small groups when conversation interest them	What's Outside, Collecting	
Listen to stories with increasing interest and recall	Be a Storyteller, Re-jig a Familiar Story	
Describe main story settings, events and principle characters	The Three Billy Goats Gruff, Build-a-Story, Picture Stories	
Question why things happen, and give explanations	What does this do?, Swapping Stories	
Initiate a conversation, negotiate positions, pay attention to and take account of others' views	Transport, Post Delivery Person	
Enjoy listening too and using spoken and written language, and readily turn to it in their play and learning	Act-a-Story, Run, Run - The Gingerbread Man, Make one like it	
Sustain attentive listening, responding to what they have heard by relating comments, questions or actions	What can it be?, Which came next?, Pass the Toy	
Listen with enjoyment, and respond to stories, songs and other music, rhymes and poems and make up their own stories, rhymes and poems	Copy me, Make Musical Instruments, Make a New Rhyme	
Use familiar words, often in isolation, to identify what they do and do not want	What's under here?, Collecting	
Use vocabulary focused on objects and people who are of particular importance to them	Tell us about..., Where can Bear go?	
Build up vocabulary that reflects the breadth of their experiences	How would I feel?, What's Outside	
Begin to experiment with language describing possession	Tell us about...	
Extend vocabulary especially by grouping and naming	Collecting, What does this do?	
Use vocabulary and forms of speech that are increasingly influenced by experience of books	Guess what it is, Feel free Book	
Extend their vocabulary, exploring the meanings and sounds of new words	Make a Call, What does this do?	

Stepping stone	Activities which address stepping stones	Comments
Use isolated words and phrases and/or gestures to communicate with those well known to them	Who shall I be?, What can it be?	
Begin to use more complex sentences	Pass the Toy, Guess what	
Use a widening range of words to express or elaborate ideas	What is it?, Pass the Toy	
Link statements and stick to a main theme or intention	What is it?, Pass the Toy	
Consistently develop a simple story, explanation or line of questioning	Taking Turns, Simply a Story	
Use language for an increasing range of purposes	Guess what, Make and Play	
Confidently talk to people other than those who are well known to them	Library Visit, Wild Animal Park	
Speak clearly and audibly with confidence and control and show awareness of the listener, for example by their use of conventions such as greetings, 'please' and 'thank you'	Make a restaurant	
Engage in activities requiring hand-eye coordination	Chalk-a-line, Scribble Scribble, Sew-sew, Make a necklace	
Draw lines and circles using gross motor movements	Chalk-a-line, Scribble Scribble	
Manipulate objects with increasing control	Scribble Scribble, Controlled Scribble	
Begin to use anticlockwise movement and retrace vertical lines	Controlled Scribble, Over-copy	
Begin to form recognizable letters	Writing notes, Copy writing, Make-a-card	
Use a pencil and hold it effectively to form recognizable letters, most of which are correctly formed	Writing notes, Copy writing, Make-a-card	
Draw and paint, sometimes giving meanings to marks	Sand Writing	
Ascribe meanings to marks	Marks for Meaning, Overcopy, Writing Notes, Send an e-mail	
Begin to break the flow of speech into words	Overcopy, Taking Messages	

Communication, Language and Literacy

© Irene Yates
www.brilliantpublications.co.uk

Stepping stone	Activities which address stepping stones	Comments
Use writing as a means of recording and communicating	Keeping a writing record	
Use their phonic knowledge to write simple, regular words, and to make phonetically plausible attempts at more complex words	Have a go, Make a Sound Book, Special Writing, Watch Out!	
Attempt writing for different purposes, using features of different forms such as lists, stories and instructions	Write me a letter, Make a necklace, Special Writing, Watch Out!	
Write their own names and other things such as labels and captions and begin to form simple sentences, sometimes using punctuation	This is me, Special Writing, Watch Out!	
Listen to and join in with stories and poems, one-to-one and also in small groups	Sharing a Book, Huff Puff	
Show interest in illustrations and print in books and print in the environment	Reading Together, Choosing Books, Reading Moments, Print Walk	
Begin to be aware of the way stories are structured	Reading Together, Simply a Story	
Have favourite books	Which Book?	
Handle books carefully	Book know-how	
Suggest how the story might end	The Three Billy Goats Gruff, Building Stories	
Know information can be relayed in the form of print	Send a Letter, Reading Together	
Hold books the correct way up and turn pages	Book Know-how	
Understand the concept of a word	Book Know-how, Modelling Writing	
Enjoy an increasing range of books	Setting -up a Book Corner, Looking at Books Together	
Begin to recognize some familiar words	Whole Words, Naming Names, Shopping Trip	
Know that information can be retrieved from books and computers	Print-a-book, What does this do?	
Enjoy rhyming and rhythmic activities	Silly Words, Make a New Rhyme	

Stepping stone	Activities which address stepping stones	Comments
Distinguish one sound from another	Make Musical Instruments, What can it be?, Misfit Words	
Show awareness of rhythm and alliteration	Rhyming names, Silly Words, Stand or Move, Silly Sentences	
Recognize rhythm in spoken words	Clapping the Pattern, All Clap Hands	
Continue a rhyming string	Rhyming Names	
Hear and say the initial sound in words and know which letters represent some of the sounds	Letter Train, What does he like? Sound Box	
Hear and say initial and final sounds in words, and short vowel sounds in words	Colour Words	
Link sounds to letters, naming and sounding the letters of the alphabet	Letter Train, Sound Box, Match the Letter, I can	
Use their phonic knowledge to write simple regular words and make phonetically plausible attempts at more complex words	Have a go, Watch Out!, Re-tell a Story	
Explore and experiment with sounds, words and texts	I hear this, What's this?, Guess what it is?	
Retell narratives in the correct sequence, drawing on language patterns of stories	Re-tell a Story, Swapping Stories	
Read a range of familiar and common words and simple sentences independently	Shopping trip, Know-a-name, Whole Words, Reading Together	
Know that print carries meaning and in English, is read from left to right and top to bottom	Reading Together, Sharing Books, Shopping Trip	
Show an understanding of the elements of stories, such as main character, sequence of events, and openings, and how information can be found in non-fiction texts to answer questions about, who, why and how	What I Liked was..., Swapping Stories, Re-tell a story, Re-jig a Familiar Story	

© Irene Yates
www.brilliantpublications.co.uk

Speaking and Listening

- Perhaps the hardest thing for a child to do is to communicate when she is not sure of her language ability. It is difficult for her to think about what she wants to say, to get the words into the right order, and to communicate her expression to other children and to adults. Your undivided attention and warm responses will help the child to develop feelings of self-confidence and satisfaction. Your interaction will give the child the power she needs to develop the ability to communicate.

- It always takes two to talk, one to listen and one to speak. Everything that we do makes a difference to the child's language development. If we keep guessing what the child wants to say and saying it for her, we will make her reluctant to have a go for herself. We have to learn to become responsive, to wait and listen, and to reinforce with praise when she gets things right.

- We also need to become aware of body language, so that we can understand the cues that children are trying to give us when they are expressing their feelings or needs. The hard bit is that we often find ourselves doing all the talking, helping when it's not needed, interrupting, assuming we know what the child wants to say and leading the child where we want her to go, language-wise.

- Every child develops gradually, at her own speed, in her own way, and we have got to be aware of this at all times, remembering that we should accept her ability 'now' and help her to progress by offering unlimited opportunities for conversation.

I hear this

Learning objectives
- To listen with enjoyment
- To explore sounds

Preparation
- Have the children sitting together, ready to listen and concentrate.

What to do
- Tell the children that you are going to play a game together called 'I hear this'.
- Explain the game – you and the children take it in turns to make a sound, and the other children have to guess what it is.
- Give an example to start – 'I hear this… moo, mooo, mooooo. What can I hear?'
- When the children have guessed it is a cow, get them to take turns to think of another sound, and make it.

Extension/variation
- Make a tape-recording of different animal sounds to play to the children and let them compare how good their own sounds are with them.

Resources
- Tape recorder
- Blank cassette tape

Communication, Language and Literacy

Face to face

Speaking and Listening

• • • • • • • • • •

Resources
▪ No special requirements

Learning objectives
● To demonstrate listening skills
● To encourage children in conversation

What to do
● During informal or formal play, try to position yourself so that the child can look directly into your eyes. This is one of the simplest but most important things you can do to encourage communication. The child can then watch how your mouth forms words and watch your eyes to see what you are looking at or what feelings you are betraying.
● It is important always to talk 'with' children, not 'at' them. Let the children lead the conversation whenever possible, even when you are tempted to 'fill in' for them. If they are struggling to find the right words, prompt gently and give positive feedback as soon as they pick up the vocabulary.

Extensions/variations
● Be prepared to bend your knees a lot!
● Get down to the same level.
● Hold the children on your knees.
● Sit on the floor sometimes and let the children have the chairs.

Links to home
● Try to use these strategies in front of parents. Explain how important they are if you think you have the opportunity.

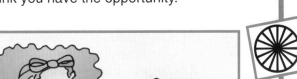

Observe, wait and listen

• • • • • • • • • •

Learning objectives
● To give opportunities for children to speak
● To encourage verbalization of ideas
● To encourage the use of talk to organize, sequence, and clarify thinking

Preparation
● Use this strategy during all play and learning situations.

What to do
● Make a mantra of the three important key words – Observe, Wait and Listen – when the children are in any speaking situation:
◆ **Observe** the child's focus of attention, facial expression and body language – this will help you to understand what the child is speaking about.
◆ **Wait** for the child to communicate first. Not always easy, but try not to control the moment by taking over.
◆ **Listen** attentively to what the child says – let the child do most of the talking; if you feel he/she needs prompting do it gently.

Extensions/variations
● Give positive feedback to speakers all the time.
● Help children to interpret ideas and feelings when they get stuck.
● Let the children lead the moment so that they can express their own feelings, needs and interests.

Multicultural links
● Be sensitive to gaps in vocabulary with children for whom English is an additional language.

Links to home
● The way you act with the children will provide a good role model for parents.

Resources
■ No special requirements

Any

© Irene Yates
www.brilliantpublications.co.uk

Show how to listen

Speaking and Listening

Resources
- No special requirements

Learning objective
● To demonstrate listening skills

What to do
● Three important concepts for helping children to develop language skills are:
  ◆ Imitate
  ◆ Interpret
  ◆ Comment
● When you imitate what the child says, she will know you are listening to her. For example, if she says 'Oh no!' and you say, 'Oh no!' as well, you interpret and you confirm that you have received the child's message. If you add, 'What's happened here?', for example, you have shown that you have guessed what the child is trying to put into words and can help her to say it. She might say, 'It's all felled down,' and you can say, 'It's all fallen down?' Repeating what the child says, with a question in your tone, will encourage the child to try again.
● Explaining that you don't understand and asking her to try again, will confirm your interest in what she has to say.
● When you comment upon what the child is doing, you are helping her to learn new vocabulary.

Extension/variation
● Look for opportunities during all activities to reinforce vocabulary and language structure.

Multicultural links
● Be sensitive to gaps in vocabulary and language structure with children for whom English is an additional language. Just comment clearly and naturally, so that the children absorb your language patterns.

Links to home
● Try to demonstrate these techniques in front of carers and parents so that they pick them up and use them themselves.

Guess what it is

Class

Learning objectives
- To listen with enjoyment
- To explore and experiment with the sounds in words

Preparation
- Have the children sitting together ready to listen and concentrate.

What to do
- Tell the children you are going to play a game called 'Guess what it is'. Look around the room and focus on an object, but don't give them too much of a visual clue to begin with because their eyes will follow yours and you want them to think about listening, not looking.
- Suppose, you had chosen 'book'. Say, 'There's something I can see that begins with the sound 'b' and ends with 'k'. Can you guess what it is?' (Make sure you do not add 'uh' to the sounds.)
- When the children have had lots of practice at the game, give them turns to work out an object of their own.

Extension/variation
- Instead of finding things in the room, think of things that the children might know and give an extra clue, for example: 'I'm thinking of something that begins with 'sh' and ends with 'p' and lives in a field.'

Resources
- No special requirements

© Irene Yates
www.brilliantpublications.co.uk

Tell us about...

Speaking and Listening

Resources
- No special requirements

Learning objectives
- To speak with confidence in front of others
- To speak clearly and audibly in front of others

Preparation
- Ask the children to take turns in bringing something from home that they would like to show to the rest of the group.

What to do
- Create a regular occasion when children from the group 'show and tell' to the rest of the children. Make simple rules, such as:
  - All children sit still, quietly and attentively to be a good audience.
  - Everyone has a turn to bring something in to the group.
  - Everyone learns to listen.
- Group the children in a way that is not threatening to the speaker, and be ready to encourage and prompt if necessary. Try not to intervene if the child who is speaking doesn't need your help. Allow her to choose her own words and verbalize her own ideas and thoughts to describe what she is showing the group.
- Work towards a situation where the group can organize and run their own 'Tell us about...' sessions independently of you, so that you are merely an observer!

Extensions/variations
- Having something to hold and show makes it easier for the child to speak in front of the group but also encourages children to talk about less concrete things, such as things they have done and events in their life, for example: being a bridesmaid, going to a wedding, having an operation, visiting the dentist, etc.
- Encourage the children to talk to the group about activities and tasks they have done in other key areas.

Class

What's under here?

Learning objective
- To use talk to clarify thinking and ideas

Preparation
- Choose an interesting large picture from an old calendar and cover it with either self-stick notes or small pieces of paper stuck on with reusable mastic adhesive.

What to do
- Put the covered picture on a wall or an easel, facing the children, and tell them that you have a 'secret' picture which you are going to uncover a little bit at a time. They are going to have to use their eyes and all their thinking skills to work out what the picture is.
- Take one self-stick note or bit of paper off and ask the children to tell you what they can see. Encourage them to verbalize as much as they can about the small amount of picture they can see – telling you the colours, whether they can see any specific thing or part of a thing, etc. Ask them to tell you what they think might be under the next bit of paper.
- Uncover the picture slowly, stimulating as much speech and vocabulary from the children as possible. When you are almost at the end ask them each to predict what they think the picture might be and why.

Extension/variation
- When the children are familiar with their written names, write them in large 'bubble writing' and cover them up in the same way, asking the children if they can predict whose name is being uncovered from the letters they can see as you remove each bit of paper (say the sounds as you uncover each letter).

Links to home
- Ask parents to donate their used, large calendars to you as calendars often have really good pictures that link with many of the areas of learning.

Resources
- Old calendars
- Self-stick notes
- Bits of paper
- Reusable mastic adhesive
- Easel (optional)

Guess what

Speaking and Listening

. . . .

Resources
- Toys and other small play equipment

Learning objectives
- To use spoken language to clarify ideas
- To develop vocabulary of description

What to do
- Explain the game to the children. The person who is 'it' has to think of something and give information about it. The rest of the group have to try and find out what the 'it' person is thinking of.
- Give the children an example first. Say something like, 'I'm thinking of something and we have some in this room. You can pick it up and walk round with it. It's white and it's made out of plastic. Sometimes you talk in it and sometimes you listen to it. The ones we have in this room are for pretending games. You might have one at home. The one at home has a number. It begins with the sound 't', sometimes it begins with the sound 'ph'. You can talk to somebody else on it.'
- When the children guess what you are thinking of, give them turns to have a go themselves.

Extensions/variations
- Remind the children that they don't have to be able to *see* what they are thinking about, just give sensible clues (they might be thinking of a dinosaur, for instance).
- Let some of the children work in pairs if it makes it easier for them.

Making jigsaws

Learning objective
- To use talk to clarify thinking and express ideas

Preparation
- Photocopy the Jigsaw template on page 171 on to thin card. Colour them in if you wish. Cut along the heavy lines.
- It is easy to make your own puzzles. Choose big, clear pictures from the catalogues or magazines. Stick them to card to make them easy to handle. Cut the card into five or six large, irregular pieces.

What to do
- Tell the children you have made a jigsaw puzzle for them, and you can't work out how to put it back together by yourself.
- Look at the pieces of card with them and ask them to tell you everything they can see. Encourage them to describe what they think the picture might be about. If they get really stuck, point out a few cues to help them – for example, you might say, 'Look, there's a baby in a buggy and there's a mum with her hands out, do you think she could be pushing the buggy?' or whatever.
- Be ready to help them expand their vocabulary as they discuss the pieces of picture. When they have finally worked out what the picture is about, ask them to try and put it back together.
- Talk about what they can see – were they right?

Extensions/variations
- Use sticky tape on the back to stick the picture back together. Ask the children to make up a few sentences that you could scribe as a caption for it.
- Do several pictures with sentence captions, punch holes in them and tie them together to make a book. Encourage the children to share it and 'read' it with each other.

Resources
- Jigsaw template on page 171
- Old catalogues
- Magazines
- Card
- Scissors
- Glue
- Sticky tape
- Pen
- Hole punch
- String/wool

Communication, Language and Literacy

© Irene Yates
www.brilliantpublications.co.uk

What does this do?

Speaking and Listening

• • • • • • • • • •

Resources
- A computer, with keyboard, monitor, mouse and printer
- Paper for printer

Learning objectives
- To introduce the children to different parts of a computer
- To give the children words for the various parts of a computer

What to do
- The children will encounter computers in all kinds of situations, so the sooner they learn to identify some of the parts and to use computer vocabulary, the better.
- Ask the children if they know what kinds of things computers can do. They will have lots of different answers. Encourage discussion about any experiences they have of computers.
- Show the parts of the computer:
  - The monitor – tell them what it is called.
  - The screen switch – show them how it switches on the screen on and off and let them use it.
  - The printer – ask them if they know what it does. Show them where the paper goes in and ask them if they know where it comes out.
  - The keyboard – show them the letters on the keyboard. Can they name any of the letters or tell you what they sound like?
  - The mouse – move the mouse to show them how it moves the arrow around the screen. Show them how you do a left click.
- Suggest that, together, you have a go at getting up a program. Decide on a program and encourage the children to help you call it up. Encourage them to use the correct words by using them yourself. Let them click on the mouse and watch the screen to see what appears. If possible, use the printer, and watch what comes out of it.

Extension/variation
- Word process a piece of creative writing and print it.

Related activity
- Send an e-mail (see page 142)

What is it?

Learning objectives
- To use spoken language to clarify ideas
- To develop vocabulary of description

What to do
- Tell the children that you are going to play a game that is all about *describing* things. Explain that 'describing' means telling what something is like. For instance, they might describe one of the children. Ask for a volunteer who doesn't mind being 'described' and help the children to verbalize descriptive phrases or sentences about that child.

- Tell the children that you are going to play a game. The child who volunteered can be 'it' first. Everyone else has to turn round and sit with their backs to the child. Give the child a toy or piece of equipment. The child now has to describe the object in simple phrases, giving every clue she can about what she can *see*. Help the child to talk about shape, size, colour, what material it is made of.

- The other children have to guess what the object is. The first person to guess correctly is 'it' next.

Extension/variation
- Make a feely bag. Let the children touch objects inside it and describe what they can feel.

Resources
- Toys and other small play equipment
- Feely bag (a bag to put objects in; the objects need to be heard and felt, but not seen)

© Irene Yates
www.brilliantpublications.co.uk

Make musical instruments

Speaking and Listening

. . . .

Resources
- Yoghurt pots
- Sticks or dowels
- Seeds
- Pebbles
- Sticky tape
- Bottles and jars
- Water
- Milk bottle tops
- String
- Elastic bands
- Containers
- Sandpaper
- Blocks
- Glue
- Small wooden strips
- Metal objects

Learning objectives
- To practise listening closely
- To explore and experiment with sounds
- To develop auditory discrimination

What to do
- Tell the children that you are going to make a range of special musical instruments together. Show them all the items you have collected and ask them if they can think of any ideas. Treat the process as a problem-solving activity, inviting children to give their ideas and experiment to see if they work.

- Make different sounds:
  - Clap yoghurt pots together, or tap sticks together.
  - Put seeds or pebbles into one yoghurt pot. Tape a second yoghurt pot firmly to it and use as a shaker.
  - Use containers of different sizes and materials as drums.
  - Fix string or elastic bands across blocks of wood and pluck them.
  - Fill bottles and jars with different levels of water and tap with pencils or dowels.
  - Stick sandpaper to two wooden blocks and rub them together.
  - Hang eight different lengths of wood from a stick with string and pull a dowel across them.
  - Tie milk bottle tops to a dowel and shake them.
  - Tap pieces of wood and metal together.

Extensions/variations
- Can the children describe the different sounds to you?
- Can they make quiet sounds and loud sounds?
- Can they make light sounds and heavy sounds?
- Can they tell you which sound they would use for a mouse, a monster, an elephant, etc?

(2–3)

What can it be?

Learning objectives
- To practise listening closely
- To explore and experiment with sounds
- To develop auditory discrimination

Preparation
- Use the tape recorder to record lots of different sounds, such as:
  - ◆ Washing up
  - ◆ Water running
  - ◆ Envelope opening
  - ◆ Newspaper rustling
  - ◆ Sausages frying
  - ◆ Birds singing
  - ◆ Cat meowing
  - ◆ Aeroplane going overhead
  - ◆ Cars passing
  - ◆ Bicycle bell.
- There is no limit to the number of sounds that children are familiar with, without ever listening to. Leave a short gap between each sound so that they don't run into each other.
- Have the children sitting together, quietly, ready to listen and concentrate.

What to do
- Tell the children that you are going to play a special tape to them. You want them to listen very carefully and put up their hands to speak in turn to tell you what they think each sound is. Play the first sound and stop the tape at the first gap. Invite suggestions. Rewind the tape and play the sound again. Ask the children if they have changed their minds or if they have any different ideas, or has the second hearing confirmed what they thought?
- Repeat the process with the rest of the sounds.

Extensions/variations
- Take small groups of children around your setting and location and get them to listen carefully and decide upon sounds to tape for the rest of the group.
- Try to tape sounds that fit in with work you are doing in other areas.

Resources
- Tape recorder
- Blank cassette

© Irene Yates
www.brilliantpublications.co.uk

Which came next?

Speaking and Listening

● ● ● ● ● ● ● ● ●

Resources

■ A range of musical or sound instruments, such as chime bars, bells, tambour, sticks; rain-stick, shakers, triangle, etc

Learning objectives

● To practise listening closely
● To explore and experiment with sounds
● To develop auditory memory

What to do

● Make sure the children are sitting all together, ready to listen and concentrate. Have the instruments laid out in front of them.
● Tell the children that you are going to play a game where the children take turns to play the instruments. Choose a child to come to the front of the group and make a sound with the first instrument. That child sits down.
● Choose a second child. This child has to do the first sound and then her own chosen sound. The next child has to do the first sound, the second sound and then her own chosen sound, etc.
● The children will have to concentrate hard to keep the activity going. When they have lost track, begin again with different children making different choices.

Extension/variation

● Give a group of children one instrument each and build up a sequential pattern of sounds. Can the watching children then direct the orchestra so that it makes the same sequential pattern?

Related activity

● Copy me (see page 33)

Make and play

Learning objectives
- To use talk to organize, clarify and sequence ideas
- To explore vocabulary

Preparation
- Have all the materials easily accessible so that the children can see what is there and make independent choices.

What to do
- Tell the children they are all going to make a puppet, and then make up a puppet play together. Discuss what their play might be about and who their puppets might be. Help them to decide on characters.
- Each child needs a paper plate for the head of the puppet. Invite them to draw, cut and stick to make the face and the hair.
- Roll pieces of card lengthwise to make 'sticks' to fix to the back of the puppets. Help the children to choose fabric to make the puppet's clothing, fix this to the stick, which becomes the puppet's neck, with an elastic band.
- The children then hold their puppet by the stick, under its clothing, and make it perform.

Extensions/variations
- Suggest that each small group works out a little play and performs it to the rest of the group.
- Encourage the children to talk to each other, and to you, through the puppets at all opportunities.

Links to home
- Invite the parents in to see the puppet shows.

Resources
- Paper plates
- Sticky tape
- Card
- Scraps of fabric
- Wool
- Glitter
- Buttons
- Felt-tip pen
- Elastic bands
- Scissors

Communication, Language and Literacy

Fish and chips

Speaking and Listening

• • • • • • • • •

Resources
■ No special requirements

Learning objective
● To explore and experiment with rhythm

Preparation
● Teach the children the French song 'Frère Jacques' so that they are familiar with the tune.

What to do
● Explain to the children that you are going to make up your own song, fitting the words to the tune that they know. Stick to something simple, like food, to make it easy for them.
● Beat out the rhythm of the first line with sticks, four beats, and ask the children to think of words for a line that will fit.
● Do the same with the other lines.
● You should come up with a song such as:
> *Fishy fingers, fishy fingers,*
> *Chips as well, chips as well,*
> *Sausage and spaghetti, sausage and spaghetti,*
> *Beans on toast, beans on toast.*
● The children will enjoy singing their song to visitors and will be enthused to make up more.

Extension/variation
● Do this with other simple well-known tunes, such as 'Twinkle twinkle, little star', 'Three blind mice' and 'Seesaw, margery daw'.

Collecting

1–5

Learning objectives
- To use talk to organize and clarify thinking and ideas
- To extend vocabulary
- To explore the meanings and sounds of new words
- To talk about objects from nature

Preparation
- Make sure the children are dressed suitably for going outside.

What to do
- Tell the children you are going on a 'nature walk' to make a collection of natural objects which you can then display in your room.
- Encourage the children to observe and talk about what they can see around them. Collect interesting seasonal objects – for instance, conkers, acorns, blackberries in autumn, common wild flowers in summer.
- When you get back to your setting invite the children to draw the things they saw and collected. Write captions with them. Ask them to decide on the words, then help them by writing the words for them to copy or trace over. Make a display of the items and the children's work.

Extension/variation
- Make a list of all the new words the children have encountered. Read the words with them and invite individuals to do an illustration for each one. Add to the display.

Links to home
- Ask for parent helpers.

Resources
- Plastic bag
- Card
- Pencils
- Paper
- Crayons
- Felt-tip pens

 Ensure correct child : adult ratio if leaving the setting.

Communication, Language and Literacy

Copy me

Speaking and Listening

• • • • • • • • • •

Resources
- No special requirements

Learning objectives
- To listen with enjoyment
- To explore and experiment with sounds

Preparation
- Make sure the children are sitting together, ready to listen and concentrate.

What to do
- Play a clapping game where the children have to imitate your action. Explain what you want them to do. Clap once and say, 'Copy me.' Clap twice and say, 'Copy me.'
- The children have to listen to how many claps you do and count how many they are doing themselves.
- Once they can do this, begin to clap simple rhythms, such as two fast claps and one slow clap or one slow clap and three fast claps.
- Invite the children to take turns to clap a rhythm for you and the group to copy.

Extensions/variations
- Clap the children's names and get the children to practise them with you.
- Play a game where you clap a name and the children have to work out whose name it is.
- Clap specific numbers for the children to count.

Related activity
- Which came next? (see page 29)

How would I feel?

● ● ● ● ● ● ● ● ● ●

Any

Learning objectives
● To speak clearly and audibly with confidence and control
● To use talk to organize and clarify feelings

Preparation
● You will need to think of some scenarios prior to the session (see below).
● Have the children sitting together, ready to listen and concentrate.

What to do
● Tell the children that you are going to tell them some little stories and you would like to see what they think of them.

● Give them various little scenarios that you would like them to respond to. For example, say, 'Just imagine – it's the weekend and you have asked your best friend to come and play at your house. You've been waiting and waiting for her to come. You've thought of all the games you can play together, and got all your toys out. Then, just before she's supposed to arrive, her mummy phones and says they can't come! Make a face that *shows* me how you would feel. Now stand up and *show* me how you feel.'

● After the children have all acted out their feelings, sit them down again (you might have to tell them to stop feeling sad now), and ask for volunteers to *tell* what they felt like.

● Go through the process with different scenarios – getting an unexpected present, going somewhere you never thought you would be able to go, somebody you love coming when you didn't expect it, etc – and get the children to put their feelings into words.

Extensions/variations
● Use paper plates to make expressive faces.
● Use puppets to act through the scenarios, with the children verbalizing the puppets' thoughts and feelings.

Resources
■ Paper plates
■ Drawing implements
■ Puppets

Communication, Language and Literacy

Make a call

Speaking and Listening

• • • • • • • • •

Resources
- Old telephones
- Discarded mobiles
- Tape recorder
- Blank cassette tape

Learning objectives
- To give opportunities to take turns in conversation
- To give opportunities to ask questions and respond
- To explore vocabulary

Preparation
- Have telephones and mobiles in all areas of play, including outside play, so that they are accepted as a normal part of all activities.

What to do
- Suggest scenarios in which the children might have telephone conversations with each other:
  - Friends and family, seeing how people are and arranging visits
  - Doctor and patient
  - Doctor and hospital
  - Hospital and patient
  - Emergency services, reporting a fire or an accident
  - Hairdressers, making appointments, putting appointments off
  - The vet's and a pet owner
  - The garage to sort out a broken car
  - The booking office, booking tickets for a trip or a party
  - The supermarket, checking something is in stock
  - The travel agent, to book a holiday.

- You will notice endless opportunities whilst observing play and role play, for the children to take on roles and have telephone conversations with each other.

Extension/variation
- Provide a tape recorder so that the children can sometimes 'formalize' their telephone conversations and record them. When they listen to them, can they hear how they speak in a slightly different way when they are making a record?

Related activity
- Taking messages (see page 152)

What's outside?

Learning objectives
- To use talk to organize and clarify thinking and ideas
- To extend vocabulary
- To explore the meanings and sounds of new words
- To talk about the seasons

Preparation
- Make sure the children are dressed for the weather and for the location.

What to do
- Take the children outside and talk about what it feels like and what it looks like. Is it cold? Is it warm? Is it very sunny? Is the sky blue or is it cloudy? Has it been raining? How can you tell? Does anyone know what the season is called? Give the children the names of the four seasons and remind them which season you are in currently.
- Ask them if they can remember the last season. What was the temperature like? What was the weather like? What did the trees look like? Were there lots of flowers or no flowers? What were the bushes like? What kind of clothes did they wear? What did they wear on their feet?
- What do the children think the next season will be? What will it be like? What will they wear? What will they do in that season?

- Aim for the children to really think about the changing pattern of the seasons, which they may not yet have become aware of, and feed in as much vocabulary as possible.

Extensions/variations
- Make a 'Seasons' book showing all the changes the children can think of.
- Play a game where you give the children the name of a season and they have to tell you as many things about it as they can.

Resources
- An outdoor exploration area
- Paper and writing/ drawing implements (or make a book (see Making Books, pages 155–170)

© Irene Yates
www.brilliantpublications.co.uk

What's this?

Speaking and Listening

Resources
- A tin tray
- Different objects, such as keys, rubber ball, marbles, pencil, spoon, etc
- A screen or similar

Learning objectives
- To listen with enjoyment
- To explore and experiment with sounds

Preparation
- Have the children sitting together, ready to listen and concentrate.

What to do
- Put all the objects on the tray and show them to the children. Get the children to identify and name them. Let them hold the objects and feel them, if they want to.

- Put something in between the children and the tray, so that they cannot see it. Ask them to close their eyes and listen carefully. Take one of the objects and drop it on to the tray from a short height.
- Ask the children to put up their hands if they think they can identify the object from the sound it makes.
- When all the objects have been dropped, remove the screen and repeat the dropping process, with the children watching and listening.

Extensions/variations
- Try using the same objects and something of a different material to drop them on to. What difference does this make to the sounds?
- Try using the same objects and dropping them from a much higher height. Does this change the sounds?
- When the children are good at the game, try using objects that they have not identified before the dropping.

Where can Bear go?

Learning objective
- To teach specific vocabulary of position words

What to do
- Have the children sitting alltogether, with you holding the bear. Tell the children that you are going to ask them, individually, to put the bear in a special place.
- Choose a child to place the bear, for example, 'on top of something'. The child sits down and you ask the group if she is right. Choose someone else for the next go. Ask the child to place the bear, for example, 'at the side of something'. That child sits down and again you ask the group if she is right. And so on.
- Other positions to ask for are:
  - In front of
  - Behind
  - Underneath
  - Below
  - Opposite
  - Inside
  - Beside
  - At the back of
  - Across from
  - At the bottom of
  - At the top of
  - First, second, last, etc.
- Point out that some of the words or phrases mean the same thing.

- You can develop this game by asking the children if they can put the bear, for example, 'in front of one thing but behind something else', but this will require quite a bit of thought for most of the children.

Extensions/variations
- Get the children to paint pictures of the bear in its different positions.
- Write a caption for each, saying, 'Can you see Bear in front of the books?'
- Make a display and read them back with the children.

Resources
- A toy, such as a bear

Communication, Language and Literacy

Pass the toy

Speaking and Listening

● ● ● ● ● ● ● ● ● ●

Resources
■ A small selection of toys and other objects

Learning objectives
● To organize, sequence and clarify thinking
● To sustain attentive listening

Preparation
● Make sure the children are sitting quietly, in a circle, ready to listen and concentrate.

What to do
● Explain to the children that you are going to pass one of the toys or objects around the circle. The game is that each person has to say something different about the object and they have to listen hard so that they do not say something somebody else has already said.
● Give an example to begin with. If you are holding a doll say, 'This is a doll,' and pass it to the next child, who might say something like, 'It's got curly hair.' And so on.
● When the children have run out of things to say, you could ask, 'Can anybody think of anything different at all?' Help with some gentle clues if you can think of things yourself. If the object has definitely been exhausted, start with another one.

Extensions/variations
● Make the game harder by asking the children to remember and say all the things that were said before their turn, in the right order.
● Instead of a toy, use objects that you use in other areas – for example a musical instrument or a piece of maths equipment.

Related activity
● I went on a bus… (see page 40)

I went on a bus...

Any

Learning objective
● To develop auditory memory

Preparation
● Have the children sitting together, ready to listen and concentrate.

What to do
● This game is a variation on 'I went shopping...' in that it begins, 'I went on a bus and out of the window I saw...'. You can begin the list yourself, the child who comes next has to say your item and then choose and add an item of her own.
● The children take turns to add something they might have seen to the list, trying to remember everything that has been mentioned and not miss anything out. When the children lose track and the list breaks down, start again with someone new and a new choice.

Extensions/variations
● This game can go on ad infinitum really, all you have to do is think up new ideas to start it off, for example:
   ◆ *For my birthday I would like...*
   ◆ *At the zoo there is a...*
   ◆ *At the toy shop I saw...*
● Play a game of things the children can do with different parts of their bodies, *I can...*

Resources
■ No special requirements

...and out of the window I saw a cat, a horse, a house ...and a tractor!

Communication, Language and Literacy

Playing with Rhyme

- Rhyme is important to children because it is really 'playing with language'. All play has great power and can provide children with excellent opportunities for developing the skills of communication. Language play not only develops the skills of communication but helps the children to understand what is real and what is not, as well as what is nonsense and what is not, and gives them opportunities to experience what is pleasurable and what is great fun in language.

- Nursery rhymes are important because they give the children the confidence to enjoy this kind of language play. It is well researched that children who have plenty of nursery rhyme experience find learning to read easier than children who have none. This is largely felt to be because there is a greater ability to understand how language works – through learning, reciting and singing nursery rhymes the children have absorbed many of the rules of speech rhythms and patterns that they will need when they start reading. They will also have a greater knowledge of the *sounds* of words, which will be a great help when they come to learn letters.

- Often, children who are too shy to speak in front of a group, or even with other children and adults on a one-to-one basis, will be able to join in the singing or saying of a nursery rhyme without any problem. By building on this you can sometimes encourage them to brave the big, wide world of language in other ways.

- All cultures have sets of folk stories, rhymes and songs. Try to build up a large repertoire and particularly try to use rhymes and songs from other cultures where it is possible and appropriate. You can, of course, provide translations, but it doesn't really matter if the children do not understand the words they are singing. If they are making the right pattern of sounds they are beginning to widen their language horizons and will enjoy using their voices and tongues as instruments.

Hey Diddle Diddle

Learning objectives
- To respond to rhymes in creative ways
- To link language with movement

Preparation
- Teach the children the nursery rhyme (see page 186 for words).

What to do
- Say the nursery rhyme very slowly. Ask the children to curl up in a ball and listen out for when you say 'The cat and the fiddle'. At this point they should uncurl and stretch themselves into cat shapes, and prowl like cats. When you get to 'The cow jumped over the moon', encourage them to leap on all fours to show the cow jumping over the moon. For the dish and the spoon, ask them in pairs to hold each other's hands and dance together on the spot.

Extension/variation
- Paint pictures of the rhyme and make a display of them.

Resources
- For words to nursery rhyme see page 186
- Space
- Paper
- Paints
- Paintbrushes

Communication, Language and Literacy

© Irene Yates
www.brilliantpublications.co.uk

Little Miss Muffet

Playing with Rhyme

• • • • • • • • • •

Resources
- For words to nursery rhyme see page 185
- Space
- Drum or tambour

Learning objective
- To respond to a rhyme in creative ways

Preparation
- Teach the children the nursery rhyme (see page 185 for words).

What to do
- Suggest the children act out the rhyme. Practise each movement first. Begin with them sitting on the floor, cross-legged. Encourage them to make exaggerated scooping and eating movements, to show Miss Muffet eating the curds and whey.
- To practise being spiders, get the children to curl up as small as they can, then to open themselves up into spidery shapes. Have them practise scurrying along the floor, on hands and feet, as spiders. They can also practise running away on tiptoes as Miss Muffet.
- Make a slow, rhythmic beat on the tambour as you say the words, encouraging the children to act out their parts as you recite.

Extensions/variations
- Watch out for children who have trouble following the beat of the percussion and give them extra help.
- Help the children to do controlled movements.
- Suggest the children take turns at being the spider and Miss Muffet.

Any

Finger rhymes

• • • • • • • • • •

Any

Learning objectives
● To explore and experiment with rhymes and movement
● To encourage awareness of the sounds in words and confidence in playing with language
● To link rhyme with movement

Preparation
● Make sure all the children are sitting where they can hear and see you.

What to do
● Introduce new rhymes to the children without the actions, then add the actions, talking through them as you go (eg, 'Here's Incy Wincy climbing up the drainpipe.'). Go through the words and actions slowly, again, encouraging the children to join in and copy. Repetition is the name of the game!

Extension/variation
● Keep adding to the children's repertoire.

Multicultural link
● Invite parents of English as Another Language (EAL) children to teach a familiar rhyme to the group, using sound and movement.

Links to home
● Invite parents in for an 'Action rhyme session'. This will help parents to learn the same words and actions, so that the children can repeat them often at home.

Resources
■ Rhymes from pages 180 to 186

Communication, Language and Literacy

Taking turns

Playing with Rhyme

• • • • • • • • • •

Resources
■ A set of as many question-asking rhymes as you can think of – eg 'Tommy Thumb'; 'Pussy-cat, Pussy-cat'; 'One, two, three, four, five', etc (see pages 180–186)

Learning objectives
● To learn and recite rhymes
● To develop an understanding of how conversation works

Preparation
● Introduce the children to the rhymes you are going to use at different times.

What to do
● Tell the children you are, together, going to sing, or say, some rhymes that ask questions and give answers. Suggest that some of the group ask the questions and the others provide the answers.

● Choose the two groups. Help the children to sing or say the rhymes, taking appropriate turns.

Extensions/variations
● Ask the children if they noticed which words rhymed in each rhyme.
● Swap the groups over and help the children to remember whether they are now questioners or responders.

Silly words

Class

Learning objectives
- To listen to and identify rhyming sounds
- To explore and experiment with the sounds in words

Preparation
- Have the children sitting together ready to listen and concentrate.

What to do
- Tell the children you are going to play a game called 'Silly words'. You are going to say a word and they are going to tell you as many words as they can think of that *sound* the same *at the end*. Give an example, such as *blow* and *grow*. Examine the sounds of the words with the children, ask which bit sounds the same and which bit sounds different. Give another word that rhymes, such as *toe*. Again, check the understanding of which bit sounds the same and which bit sounds different.
- Ask the children to give you as many more words as they can think of, ending with the sound of 'ow' (as in *cow*). When they have run out of 'real' words, encourage them to make up 'silly' words.

Extensions/variations
- Explain to the children that when words sound the same at the end, we say that they *rhyme*, and we call them *rhyming* words.

- Ask the children for other examples of rhyming words that they know.
- Play this game with different sounds, many, many times.
- Make the game appropriate to activities you are working on in other key areas by choosing words about what you are doing, for instance if you are cooking you might begin with *bake* and *cake*.

Related activity
- Rhyming names (see page 56)

Some rhyming, one-syllable sounds to use are:	
ai	grey, pray
er	fir, fur
air	chair, hair
ee	bee, tea
ear	here, fear
ie	by, dry
ake	cake, bake
or	four, door
oa	toe, grow
ow	cow, sound
ab	crab, dab
ib	crib, fib
ob	job, mob
ack	jack, snack
ike	like, bike

Resources
- No special requirements

Communication, Language and Literacy

Playing with Rhyme

• • • • • • • • • •

Resources
- Space

Learning objectives
- To listen and respond to songs and rhymes
- To make up own words to songs and rhymes
- To link rhyme with movement

Preparation
- Teach the rhyme:

> *We all clap hands together*
> *We all clap hands together*
> *We all clap hands together*
> *As children like to do.*

What to do
- Arrange the children in a circle, standing or sitting in a space. Ask the children to give examples of things they might do instead of clapping hands. Give individual children opportunities to make up a verse of the rhyme. Encourage them to think of things they haven't chosen before – *stamp our feet, stand up, twirl round, shrink down small, reach up tall, roll our hands, tiptoe round*, etc.

Extensions/variations
- Give the children the opportunity to take turns in being leader and deciding what to do next.
- Use the rhyme to practise different forms of movement, direction, etc.

Make a new rhyme

Any

Learning objective
● To respond to known rhymes and create own variations

Preparation
● Practise reciting or singing a well-known rhyme with the children.

What to do
● Suggest that it would be fun for the group to make up their own rhyme. Begin just by changing the rhyming word – eg 'star' – and encourage the children to think of ways of making the wording appropriate. For instance, they might come up with:

> *Twinkle, twinkle, little car*
> *How I wonder where you are*
> *Far away where it is night*
> *With your headlights shining bright*
> etc.

● When they have the idea of doing this, encourage them to begin with new words that don't rhyme with 'star'. Then lose the 'twinkle, twinkle' bit, until you end up with a totally different rhyme, using only the rhythm of the original.

● You will need to work on several sessions to develop the children's ideas this far.

Extensions/variations
● Make posters showing your new rhymes and help the children to 'read' and recite them.
● Make a book of your own new nursery rhymes.
● Choose a rhyme as your base model which ties in with something you are doing in other areas, for instance if you are looking at numbers try and make up different words to 'Two, four, six, eight…'.

Resources
■ A rhyme the children know well, such as 'Twinkle, twinkle little star' (see pages 180–186)
■ Flip chart
■ Pen

Communication, Language and Literacy

Picture pairs

Playing with Rhyme

• • • • • • • • • •

Resources
- Rhyming pairs template on page 172
- Magazines, cards, catalogues, etc, that can be cut up
- Scissors
- Card
- Glue
- Felt-tip pen

Learning objective
● To reinforce understanding of 'rhyme'

Preparation
● Photocopy the template on page 172 on to thin card. It could be coloured in first. Laminating or covering with sticky back plastic will increase its life. Cut out the cards.

What to do
● Spread all of the cards in front of the children. Go through the cards with the children, making sure that they all know what each one shows. Turn the cards face down. The children take turns to turn over a card and say its name, then turn over another one and identify that, too. If the words rhyme, the child takes the pair. The child with the most pairs at the end of the game is the winner. If there are any pictures over the winner can decide which set they belong to and win those, too.

Extension/variation
● Ask the children to help you look for more pictures (from magazines, cards, catalogues, etc) which you can add to the game.

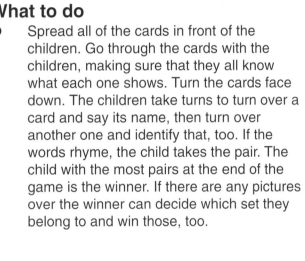

Stand or move

3–5

Learning objectives
- To reinforce knowledge and understanding of rhyme
- To give opportunity to link language and movement
- To develop listening and thinking skills

Preparation
- You need to have done some work on rhyming sounds before this activity.

What to do
- The children need to be in a large space, standing so that they can turn around without touching anyone else.
- Explain that you are going to play a game called 'Stand or Move'. Choose a word together, for example, *cat*. Explain that you are going to call out a word that might or might not rhyme with that word. If the word you call out rhymes then the children must move on their spot. If the word doesn't rhyme they must freeze and stand still. Encourage all kinds of on-the-spot moving and shape-making, but if they move and the word doesn't really rhyme they will be 'out'. If the word does rhyme but they stand still they will be 'out'. Call out a series of words until you've exhausted your ideas, then change the focus word to something else.

Extension/variation
- Encourage children to have individual turns at being the caller. You will need to be close by to support them.

Related activity
- Silly words (see page 46)

Resources
- Large space

© Irene Yates
www.brilliantpublications.co.uk

What's your favourite?

Playing with Rhyme

• • • • • • • • • • •

Resources
- Computer
- Word-processing program
- Printer
- Paper
- Nursery rhyme (see pages 180–186)
- Computer gallery of pictures (optional)

Learning objective
- To use the computer to print out a favourite nursery rhyme

What to do
- Suggest to the children that you make a printed copy of one of their favourite rhymes. Give plenty of time and discussion to choosing a rhyme that all the group want to reproduce.
- Type in the rhyme, getting the children to help you when you can. For instance, they may be able to help you type in the title. Choose a large, clear font with letters that the children can discriminate.
- When it is all typed in, ask the children to help you to 'read' it back, to make sure there are no mistakes. Read the rhyme with the children, pointing to the words. Show the children how to 'save'.
- With the children's help, print out the rhyme, getting them to do as much of the task as possible, such as pointing the mouse, clicking, etc.
- Read the printed rhyme together.

Extensions/variations
- If you have the facility, illustrate the rhyme with pictures from the computer gallery.
- Print a different rhyme for each group of children and put them together to make a book.

① – ④

Clapping the pattern

Learning objectives
- To introduce the idea of sound patterns
- To develop an understanding of syllables

What to do
- Tell the children that you are going to clap somebody's name. They need to listen very carefully to see if they can work out who it is. Clap your own name. Give the children opportunities to decide whose name it is. Repeat the clapping each time someone gets it wrong. Watch the children's faces to see who understands and who does not. Tell them it is your name. Clap it again with them listening. Ask them to clap with you.
- Repeat the process, using a child's name. Repeat again. Ask for a volunteer to clap his/her own name. Do the children all agree with the clapped pattern? Play this game often.

Extensions/variations
- When the children have a really good idea of clapping a rhythm, clap a nursery rhyme that they know well, for them to identify.
- Clap a chosen rhyme together.

Related activity
- Copy me (see page 33)

Resources
- No special requirements

© Irene Yates
www.brilliantpublications.co.uk

Do these words rhyme?

Playing with Rhyme

• • • • • • • • • •

Resources
- Card
- Pictures from magazines
- Pen

Learning objectives
- To identify rhyming words
- To give practice in finding rhymes and identifying non-rhyming words

Preparation
- Arm yourself with lists of words that rhyme. To each list of rhyming words, add one word that doesn't rhyme (see examples in the box).
- Children should be sitting quietly and ready to listen.

What to do
- Say the words clearly and slowly to the children and ask them to identify the word which doesn't fit the rhyming pattern.
- Make sure you don't always give the rhyming and non-rhyming words in the same order. Also, stick to short, one-syllable words, but vary the way you make them 'not rhyme'. For instance, you may have the same middle vowel, but a different sound ending, or you may have a completely different vowel sound and the same ending.

Extension/variation
- Give the children the set of rhyming words and ask for volunteers to give you words that don't rhyme. Ask the children if they can find rhyming words for the new 'non-rhyming' words.

Lists you could use (the non-rhyming words are underlined):

cat, hat, <u>dot</u>, mat

by, fly, tie, <u>tin</u>

toe, no, <u>note</u>, row

sea, <u>ship</u>, flea, tree

day, play, <u>why</u>, say

hair, bear, pear, <u>pin</u>

door, four, paw, <u>rain</u>

boy, toy, <u>girl</u>, joy

slow, grow, toe, <u>tooth</u>

blue, threw, shoe, <u>ball</u>

track, back, <u>front</u>, Jack

lob, sob, <u>dish</u>, rob

Echoes

Any

Learning objectives
- To introduce the idea of sound patterns
- To develop an understanding of syllables

What to do
- Have the children sitting in front of you and ask them to take turns. Clap a simple pattern and the child whose turn it is claps it back to you. When everyone has had a turn, let them take turns to clap a pattern and choose someone to clap an echo back to them.

Extensions/variations
- Clap out simple phrases – for example: 'How are you today?' – for the children to try and guess what the phrase is.
- Clap the rhythms of other rhymes and songs that the children know.

Related activities
- Copy me (see page 33)
- Clapping the pattern (see page 52)

Resources
- No special requirements

Communication, Language and Literacy

Playing with Rhyme

• • • • • • • • • •

Resources

■ The words to the song 'Here we go round the mulberry bush, (see page 185)

Learning objectives
● To link language with physical movement
● To teach names of body parts

Preparation
● Teach the children to sing the song. The way the game is played is that the children go round in a circle as they are singing the first two lines. Then they stop, facing inward to do the action. Repeat as often as you wish.

What to do
● You can teach the children the names of actions and of body parts while they are playing this game.
● Give the children lots of different actions, on each occasion that you play the game (but not all at once!). For example:
  ◆ *We wash our faces*
  ◆ *We clean our teeth*
  ◆ *We comb our hair*
  ◆ *We shrug our shoulders*
  ◆ *We wave our hands*
  ◆ *We fold our arms*
  ◆ *We stick out our tongues*
  ◆ *We hang our heads*
  ◆ *We twist our wrists*
  ◆ *We wriggle our fingers*
  ◆ *We pat our knees*
  ◆ *We point our toes*
  ◆ *We point our elbows*
  ◆ *We stand on our heels*
  ◆ *We raise our eyebrows*.

Extensions/variations
● Use actions like digging, jumping, climbing, tiptoeing, etc, to give the children opportunities for doing big movements.
● Use actions like smiling, crying, being angry, so that the children can get used to making different facial expressions.

(6–8)

Rhyming names

Class

Learning objectives
● To explore sounds in words
● To play with the idea of rhyme

Preparation
● You need to have introduced the children to the idea of rhyme before you play this game.
● Prior to the activity, look at a list of the children's names and think of words that rhyme. The rhymes don't have to 'make sense' as long as they help children to get the idea of rhyming.

What to do
● The idea of the game is to find, or make up, words which will rhyme with a child's name. If your own name is easy to rhyme, use it as your demonstration – eg 'My name is Mrs. Jones and it rhymes with Mrs. Bones', so that children get the idea. Explore the children's names. If their first name hasn't a word that rhymes with it, perhaps their middle name does, or their end name. If none of the names is easy to rhyme, encourage the children to find as many different beginning sounds as they can, until they find a rhyme that they think is suitable, or funny enough.

Extensions/variations
● At the end of the game, see how many of the rhyming names the children can remember and recite.
● Take opportunities to make 'mistakes' and call the children 'accidentally' by the chosen rhyming name when you are working on other things.

Related activity
● Silly words (see page 46)

"My name is Amber and it rhymes with clamber!"

Playing with Rhyme
● ● ● ● ● ● ● ● ● ●

Resources
■ No special requirements

Communication, Language and Literacy

Weather report

Playing with Rhyme

• • • • • • • • • •

Resources

- For words of 'I hear thunder' see page 180
- Paper
- Writing/drawing implements
- Percussion instruments

Learning objectives

- To learn and sing a rhyme
- To put actions to the rhyme
- To think of weather words

Preparation

- Teach the children the nursery rhyme (see page 180 for words).

What to do

- Have the children standing in a circle, to sing the rhyme. Their actions should be:
  - ◆ Nothing for the first line
  - ◆ A hand behind their ear than hands open for the second line
  - ◆ Fingers wiggling in the air for the 'pitter patter' of the raindrops
  - ◆ Stomping their feet for the end of the rhyme.
- Ask the children to try to think of other words for raining. Encourage them to think of the rain when it is really pouring down, when it is drizzling, when it is teeming. Can they fit those words into the rhyme in place of 'pitter patter'?
- Ask the children to think of words for the thunder. Encourage them to think of loud noise words that describe the thunder: *boom*, *clash*, *bang*, *thump*, for instance.

Extensions/variations

- Be aware of children who are frightened of thunderstorms.
- Draw weather pictures and label them.
- Make a weather book showing different kinds of weather.
- Use percussion instruments to create sounds to go with the song.

Role Play

- In a way, role play is a way of practising by doing. It allows the children to be anyone, to go anywhere in both time and space, and to do anything.

- The greatest tool that children have to help them develop, not just their language skills, but in every way, is their imagination. Unfortunately, much of the material that is provided for children to play with actually detracts from, rather than adds to, imagination. A brightly coloured plastic cooker, for example, can be great if you want to play at being a cook – for a while. Then, when you no longer want to be cook, the plastic cooker is still a plastic cooker. A cardboard box, on the other hand, can be anything you want it to be. You just give it a name and let your imagination take wing. The great thing about playing with cardboard boxes is that the children have to improvise – and the improvisation sharpens their imagination, developing their language at the same time as they think, problem-solve and negotiate.

- Role play offers the most tremendous range of experiences – from real-life or from history, the future, the animal kingdom, or whatever. It is an excellent way to learn vocabulary and to learn how to put words together, negotiating and interacting with your fellow role modellers – and it is tremendously fulfilling and pleasurable into the bargain.

- Role play is a way of participating, of feeling empathy, of identifying oneself with others, and of communicating in verbal and nonverbal ways. It is a way of learning about feelings – and a way of experiencing different reactions.

- Use role play to recreate experiences that the children may have had that are not happy ones, be sensitive in your approach and help the children to come to terms with things that have happened.

- Role play is also a useful tool for practising something that is *going* to happen – a group trip, for example, where you want the children to understand what is expected of them when you take them outside of your setting.

- The suggestions given in this section are just that – only suggestions. You are not expected to stick to them unquestioningly, rather to use them as jumping-off points for engaging your own, and the children's, imagination in a way that will lead to vocabulary extension and language enrichment.

© Irene Yates
www.brilliantpublications.co.uk

Wild animal park

Role Play

• • • • • • • • • • •

Resources
- Soft toys
- Paper
- Card
- Scissors
- Felt-tip pens
- Cardboard boxes
- String
- Silvery foil
- Cling film
- Dowel or stick
- Reference books about animals
- Lots of space

Learning objectives
- To use language to imagine and recreate roles and experiences
- To extend vocabulary
- To explore written and spoken language

Preparation
- Discuss the idea of a 'wild animal park' and invite the children to tell you any wild animal park or zoo experiences they have had, what they think a wild animal park is for and what kind of animals they might see there.
- Ask the children to bring in any animal toys they might like to lend to the group's wild animal park (make sure they are labelled clearly with owners' names).

What to do
- Ask the children to sort the toys into sets – elephants, lions, monkeys, seals, etc. Make a habitat for each set, using cardboard boxes for sleeping quarters or pens. If you are short of certain species, draw them on card, colour them and cut them out.
- Make fish out of card and stick silvery scales to them. Cut out the sides of a box and fill in the spaces with cling film to make an aquarium. Suspend the fish with cotton from a stick or dowel across the box.

- Make labels and captions for each set of animals, for example:
  - ◆ Do not feed the monkeys!
  - ◆ Don't poke the lion!
  - ◆ Come back to feed the seals at 3 o'clock!
- Make entrance tickets for the children to sell and buy.
- Make a display of the reference books for the children to search for information.

Extensions/variations
- Make a 'Wild Animal Park' book.
- Tape record stories about the wild animals.
- Take lots of photos so that you can discuss the project with the children when it has finished.
- Give the children opportunities to address the group, talking about what they have done.

Links to home
- Invite parents to visit your wild animal park.

3–4

Dressing up box

Learning objectives
- To use language to imagine and recreate roles and experiences
- To extend vocabulary
- To explore written and spoken language
- To interact with others, negotiate plans and activities

Preparation
- Make sure the dressing up box is always easily available. Hang the jewellery on the mug holder.

What to do
- Encourage the children to sort through the dressing up box to find items they want to wear, independently whenever they feel like it.
- Give lots of positive feedback – ask the children when they are dressed up, 'Oh, who has come to visit us this morning? Where have you been? Where are you going?' and encourage them to have conversations with you, in role, and with other adults in the group – but only if they want to. You have to be careful not to intervene too much and break the spell.

Extension/variation
- Dressing up games are often continuous – the children have a phase of dressing up and playing a certain role for a length of time and then get fed up with it and move on to something else when they have 'played it out'. Let this happen as a natural course of events.

Link to home
- Ask parents if they can supply any bits and pieces for your dressing up box.

Resources
- Large cardboard box
- Clothing items
- Shoes
- Jewellery
- Mug holder
- Hats

Communication, Language and Literacy

www.brilliantpublications.co.uk

Build a den

Role Play

• • • • • • • • • •

Resources

- Fabric such as an old sheet
- Big piece of furniture (eg table, large piece of play equipment)
- Cushions
- Building blocks
- Throw and/or rug
- Cardboard boxes
- Old telephone
- Resources for picnic (either pretend or real)

Learning objective

- To give opportunities for organizing, sequencing and clarifying ideas through talk

Preparation

- You need only to find a corner where the children may build the den – it will help if there is a big piece of furniture by one of the walls so that the children can balance the sheet on it to make a roof. If they are building it outside, a garden table or large piece of play equipment might help.

What to do

- Tell the children that you would like them to build a 'good den' in the corner you have designated for it. Tell them they can be anyone they like to build the den. They might want to be soldiers, explorers, people on holiday – whatever. Give them all the materials you have collected and just let them get on with it. Suggest that they come to you only if they need something else or have a problem they just cannot resolve between them.
- When the den is built ask if you may visit it. Encourage them to ask you in and describe the various parts of it and tell you who they are (the role they are playing) and what they are doing there.

Extensions/variations

- Ask the children if there is anything else they need to improve their den.
- Give the children the opportunity to return to the same play another day, until you feel they have exhausted it. Often their dens will get more sophisticated over time, until they run out of steam.
- Give the children resources to 'picnic' in the den (either pretend or real).

Acting stories

Learning objectives

3–5

- To develop language for interaction and expression
- To retell stories in action
- To develop problem-solving skills

Preparation

- Choose a story the children know well. Recap the main events of the story with the children.

What to do

- After discussing the story, assign roles and props/costume items to the children and suggest that they act out the story for you.
- Find a quiet corner, sit to watch, listen and observe. Talk them through their ideas for problem-solving carefully so that they can decide whether their ideas will work or not. (For instance, if they are acting out 'The three billy goats gruff' they may want to build something that represents a bridge. Their ideas may lead them to put chairs together – not a good idea! Guide them to see that the bridge can be imagined from laying something flat on the floor.)
- Only intervene when absolutely necessary: the children will hit obstacles in their re-enactments but will develop their problem-solving and thinking skills by overcoming them.

Extension/variation

- Sometimes re-enactments turn into 'favourite games' for a while. If this happens, encourage the children to swap roles and see/act the story from every perspective.

Related activity

- The Three Billy Goats Gruff (see page 115)

Resources

- A bank of the children's known stories (see pages 187–191 for simple story lines)
- Collect or make items of costume or props to help them to extend their imaginations

© Irene Yates
www.brilliantpublications.co.uk

Set up a fish 'n' chip shop

Role Play

• • • • • • • • • •

Resources
- Cardboard boxes
- Scissors
- Cling film or cellophane
- Coloured paper
- Card (lots)
- Glue
- Till
- Paper hats
- Aprons
- Plastic utensils
- Paper for wrapping

Learning objectives
- To talk and explore language through the process of making the fish and chip shop
- To develop language for thinking and problem-solving

Preparation
- Talk about the local fish and chip shop. What can the children tell you about it? Suggest making your own fish and chip shop in a corner of the room.

What to do
- With the children's help, make the fish and chip shop. Make a counter from a cardboard box or table. Have two big cardboard boxes as friers, one to cook the fish in, one to cook the chips in. Make a microwave oven by cutting the front of a box so that it opens. Cut out a 'window' and cover it with cling film or cellophane. Get the children to make some switches to stick on.
- Make the fish, chips and other food items out of card – you will need lots!

- Ask the children to suggest notices, labels and signs you will need:
  - Open/Closed
  - Frying now
  - Fish 'n' chips
  - Pies and burgers
  - A price list.
- Write them with the children dictating to you, so that they can see the writing process in action. Encourage the children to 'write' their own labels, too.

Extensions/variations
- Make the fish and chip shop a part of everyday play.
- Set up a burger bar or a pizzeria in the same way.
- Give the children opportunities to talk about their experiences.

Related activities
- Fish and chips (see page 31)
- Make a restaurant (see page 64)

Communication, Language and Literacy

Make a restaurant

3–4

Learning objectives
- To use language to imagine and recreate roles and experiences
- To extend vocabulary
- To explore written and spoken language

Preparation
- Talk to the children about how a restaurant works, what it's for, where the children have been, what kinds of restaurants there are.

What to do
- You need cardboard boxes, turned upside-down to be tables, and cardboard boxes with no top and one of the four sides cut away, to be chairs. Set up as many tables and chairs as your restaurant will take.
- Make plates and cutlery out of card. Place a yoghurt pot in the centre of each table with some cut out and coloured card flowers in.
- Make a menu on a large piece of card or a board, to go on the wall. Invite the children to suggest items that might be on the menu, and scribe them, reading them back with the children.
- Help the children to decide who will be guests and who will be waiters to start the play. Equip the waiters with notebooks (make them out of small pieces of paper stapled together) and pencils to take the orders.

- If space and imagination permit, make cookers for one or two chefs and make pans and food out of card.
- Get the children who are visiting the restaurant to take time dressing up, ready to go out for a meal.

Extensions/variations
- Make a fast food restaurant.
- Give the children lots of opportunities for talking about what they have been doing and playing.
- Make some real food and drinks to serve at the restaurant.

Links to home
- Invite parents to visit the restaurant.

Related activity
Set up a fish 'n' chip shop (see page 63)

Resources
- Corrugated cardboard
- Paper
- Card
- Scissors
- Felt-tip pens
- Cardboard boxes
- Yoghurt pots
- Glue
- Toy cutlery and canteen/table equipment if available
- Stapler
- Pencils

Communication, Language and Literacy

© Irene Yates
www.brilliantpublications.co.uk

Build a castle

Role Play

• • • • • • • • • •

Resources

- Reference books about castles
- Corrugated cardboard
- Paper
- Card
- Scissors
- Felt-tip pens
- Cardboard boxes
- Hole punch
- String
- Blue curtain/sheet
- Tin foil
- Fabric
- Lots of space

Learning objectives

- To use language to imagine and recreate roles and experiences
- To extend vocabulary
- To explore written and spoken language

Preparation

- Look at some reference books with the children about castles, knights in armour, jousts, etc.
- Ask the children to tell you any experiences they have had of visiting castles, ruined or otherwise, and to tell you what they know of castles from programmes, films or videos they may have seen.

What to do

- Suggest to the children that you could build your very own medieval castle. Use corrugated cardboard to make walls against one of the setting's walls. Cut the top of the castle walls to make crenellated parapets or ramparts.
- Make a drawbridge by joining one end of a large piece of card to a space in the castle walls. Tie string to the other end and punch holes at this end and in the two walls. Put string through the holes and use it to pull the drawbridge up and down. Make a moat with an old blue curtain or sheet. Make turrets by rolling up corrugated cardboard and cutting the tops into an appropriate shape.

- Make crowns and cover them with tin foil. Make hats by rolling thin card into a pointed shape and taping a piece of fine fabric to hang down from the point. Make breastplate armour with pieces of card, cover with foil and punch a hole in each of the four corners. Thread string through and secure across the child's back.
- Make a display of books about castles which are accessible to the children and encourage them to share the books with each other and other adults. Give the children as much explanation and information about castles as they can absorb and set them off to play and pretend.

Extensions/variations

- Make a 'This is our Castle' book, with pictures and words for the different parts of the castle.
- Give the children opportunities to address the group, telling how they built the castle and what they have done in it.

Office centre

Learning objective
- To give the children familiarity with technology

Preparation
- Collect together as many defunct pieces of equipment as you can, or that you have room for.

What to do
- Set up an 'office centre' as simply as you can. It doesn't need to be complicated at all – just place all the pieces of equipment you have on the tables and tell the children that this is the 'office centre'. Help them to decide what kind of office it is today – doctor's, hairdresser's, business, bank, etc.
- Show the children the message pads and pencils and discuss what they are for.
- Join in the role play, gently to begin with, helping them to identify all the pieces of equipment and know what they are pretending to do with them. Give the children plenty of time to develop their own games on their own.

Extension/variation
- If you haven't got much space, put the office centre away at the end of the day, and bring it out at different times, rather than all the time.

Links to home
- Ask parents if they have any defunct materials which you could use for your 'office'.

Resources
- Computers
- Printers
- Telephones (static and mobile)
- Fax machines
- Tables
- Chairs
- Message pads
- Paper
- Pencils
- Pens
- Rubber stamps

© Irene Yates
www.brilliantpublications.co.uk

Post delivery person

Role Play

Resources
- Post box
- Lots of letters and cards written by the children

Learning objectives
- To extend children's vocabulary and understanding
- To explore the meaning and sound of new words

Preparation
- You need to have made the post box and posted several letters or cards in it.

What to do
- Set two or three children up to be post delivery people. If you have postal worker's hats or something that makes their costume, so much the better. Provide the children with bags to put the letters and cards in.
- Help the children to open the post box and take the letters out of it. Decide who will deliver whose post.
- Help the children to sort the post, using cues such as familiar names and the beginning sounds of names.
- The children should put the letters they are delivering into their bags and set off to deliver them.

Extensions/variations
- Try to give everyone a turn at becoming a post delivery person.
- Use a cardboard box as a postal van and deliver 'parcels'.

Related activities
- Send a letter (see page 68)
- Write me a letter (see page 151)

Send a letter

Learning objectives
- To give opportunities for learning new vocabulary
- To give opportunities for showing that print has meaning

Preparation
- Talk with the children about letters, how they get from one place to another, and what you do when you've written one, to check their knowledge.

What to do
- Suggest to the children that you make a post box of the group's own. Show them the cardboard box and ask them how you can make it into a post box. Explain that the post box will need somewhere for the letters to go in when they are posted, and somewhere for the letters to come out when they are collected.
- Cut a slot in the front for the letters to go in, and make a 'door' at the back for collecting the post. Secure the door with a piece of sticky tape.

- Ask the children to help you decide on the collection times and make a label for the front of the post box and glue it on.
- Invite the children to write their letters and cards to each other. Help them by scribing for them or let them 'pretend' write, to the best of their ability. Make sure that everybody has at least one letter to receive.
- Post the letters.

Extensions/variations
- Give the children turns to collect, sort and deliver the post.
- Write a 'real' letter to the group and take the children to post it.

Links to home
- Invite the children to write letters to their families.

Related activities
- Post delivery person (see page 67)
- Send an e-mail (see page 142)
- Write me a letter (see page 151)

Resources
- Large cardboard box
- Scissors
- Sticky tape
- Paper
- Glue
- Felt-tip pen
- Writing paper or card
- Pencils

© Irene Yates
www.brilliantpublications.co.uk

Hospital corner

Role Play

• • • • • • • • • •

Resources
- Corrugated cardboard
- Paper
- Card
- Scissors
- Felt-tip pens
- Cardboard boxes
- Yoghurt pots
- Glue
- Toy medical equipment if available
- Stapler
- Pencils
- Bulldog clips
- Cushions
- Safety pins
- Towels, fabric, etc

Learning objectives
- To use language to imagine and recreate roles and experiences
- To extend vocabulary
- To explore written and spoken language

Preparation
- Talk to the children about their experiences of hospitals, eliciting as much vocabulary from them as possible.

What to do
- Suggest to the children that you set up your own hospital corner, where they, or the toys, can be patients. Invite as many ideas from them as they can come up with.
- Use corrugated cardboard to make screens, cardboard boxes with the tops cut off to make beds for the toys. Use dolls' pram and cot mattresses, pillows and blankets for the beds. A pillow, a blanket, or even a piece of cardboard, can provide a stretcher or a trolley for a sick toy.
- If the children are going to be patients, lay towels on the floor to be beds, and fold another towel or tea-towel at the bottom of the 'bed' to be a blanket.
- Make upside down watches out of card and pin them to the nurses and doctors. Cut medicine bottles and spoons out of card.
- Make patients' records with A4 paper attached with a bulldog clip to a piece of card, and put one at the bottom of each bed, with a pencil. Help the nurses and doctors to fill the charts in and write notes on each record and to write out 'prescriptions'.
- Make a cardboard box 'chair' (box with the top and one side cut out) for the side of each bed and provide a list of times that visitors may come into the ward. Make yoghurt pot flower pots for each patient.
- Make a clock for the wall and delegate one of the nurses to ring a bell or tell the visitors when they must leave.

Extensions/variations
- Make a little book of hospital words.
- Give the children lots of opportunities to talk about their real hospital experiences.
- Give opportunities for recounting imagined experiences.
- Make get-well cards for the patients.

© Irene Yates
www.brilliantpublications.co.uk

Communication, Language and Literacy

Who shall I be?

Class

Learning objectives
● To interact with others
● To recreate roles and experiences and use language to explain them

What to do
● Tell the children you are going to play a game where they have to pretend to be someone else.
● First of all, everybody sits in a space and thinks of somebody they might be (eg firefighter, window-cleaner, car driver). When everyone is sure they have a person, you start the music. While the music is playing, the children act out doing whatever their chosen person might do. When the music stops they all have to stand still in a freeze of that person.
● A child is chosen to be 'it'. Everybody else sits down and watches that child act out her person. The children have to try and work out who it is.
● The music begins again and everyone carries on acting out their person. When the music stops another child is chosen to be 'it'. And so on.

Extensions/variations
● Help the children decide on role models by suggesting a number of tasks that might be performed by various people.
● Add a 'writing' element to the activity by inviting the children to draw a picture of their chosen person and compose a caption for you to scribe.

Resources
■ Tape recorder
■ Music tape
■ Paper
■ Writing implements

Communication, Language and Literacy

Transport

Role Play

. . . .

Resources
- Corrugated cardboard
- Paper
- Card
- Scissors
- Felt-tip pens
- Cardboard boxes

Learning objectives
- To use language to imagine and recreate roles and experiences
- To extend vocabulary
- To explore written and spoken language

Preparation
- Discuss various modes of travel and invite the children to tell you their experiences of the different kinds of transport they have come into contact with.

What to do
- Choose a mode of transport that the children seem to be fairly enthusiastic about. Use as many cardboard boxes as you have available to become that kind of transport.
- You need only to draw wheels on a box for it to become a car, the children's imagination will do the rest. You can make a petrol station out of corrugated cardboard, and issue receipts for petrol. Make driving licences and tax and insurance papers for the drivers.
- A little imagination can turn the cars into aeroplanes and the petrol station into an airport. Make passports and travel documents and get the travellers to send postcards home.
- When these modes of transport have been exhausted make boats. Again, make passports and travel documents, fishing rights licences, ships' diaries, captains' notes, etc.

Extensions/variations
- Give lots of opportunities for the children to recount both their real life and their imagined experiences.
- Cut up travel brochures to make maps and information books about places to stay.
- 'Read' maps and atlases with the children.

3–4

Space shuttle

Learning objectives

(3–4)
- To use language to imagine and recreate roles and experiences
- To extend vocabulary
- To explore written and spoken language

Preparation

- Talk to the children about journeys into space and check their knowledge about space travel, rockets, shuttles, the moon, stars, planets, etc.

What to do

- Suggest to the children that you make your own space shuttle, so that they can be astronauts and travel through space. Show the children all the materials you have gathered to make the space shuttle and discuss how you can build it together, making it a problem-solving exercise. Use large sheets of corrugated cardboard against a wall as the sides, with a space cut out or folded to make an entry/exit, or docking chamber, and drape fabric or netting across the top. Roll up a piece of card and make a pointed end on it for a rocket or launcher, cover it with tin foil to give a metallic look, and secure it to the side of the shuttle.

- Inside the shuttle you need perhaps a bedchamber, a desk and chair, and any bits of old technological equipment you can get your hands on. Leave writing equipment and 'radio'-phones in the shuttle for constant use.
- Encourage the children to use 'space' language, and to practise counting backwards for 'lift-off'. When the shuttle is completed, leave them to play.

Extensions/variations

- Make a list of space words that the children know and read them with them.
- Encourage the children to send messages, verbally, in writing and in code, from space to earth.
- Make stars, a moon, and planets and stick them around the space shuttle.
- Make a 'Journey Into Space' book together.
- Give the children opportunities to address the group, talking about their experiences.

Resources

- Large sheets of corrugated card
- Fabric
- Tin foil
- Netting
- Old phones
- Old fax machines or computers
- Table
- Chair
- Writing materials
- Paints, brushes, etc

Be a pirate

Role Play

Resources
- Large cardboard box
- Paints
- Paintbrushes
- Large sheets of paper or sheet
- T-shirt
- Eye-patch
- Earring
- Painted cut-out parrot
- Treasure map
- Scarf
- 'Gold' coin
- Jolly Roger flag

Learning objectives
- To extend children's vocabulary
- To explore the meaning and sound of new words

Preparation
- Make a pirate ship out of a big cardboard box, cover a section of floor space with paper or a sheet to be a treasure island.

What to do
- Discuss with the children the meaning of 'pirate'.
- Show the children the pirate items you have made and collected. Ask the children to describe them, name them and tell you what the pirate would need them for.
- Talk about the kind of hazards pirates might face – storms at sea, sharks, huge waves, etc.
- Set off a small group of children at a time to be pirates in their pirate boat, sailing to the island to look for treasure.

Extensions/variations
- Have a plenary session where different groups of 'pirates' tell the others how they got on.
- Make up a pirate song.
- Give opportunities for discussing the experiences.

Related activities
- Message in a bottle (see page 153)
- Treasure map (see page 154)

Looking at Books

- Many children do not have access to books at home and rarely see anyone reading. If you can act as a reading role model you will go a long way towards achieving the objective of them seeing reading as a natural and enjoyable activity. In a way, this is your greatest responsibility in the development of their reading skills. If they see that you enjoy reading, and get a lot out of it, they will be motivated to do it for themselves and everything else will follow.

- The world children live in is often confusing and unpredictable. Books offer them the opportunity to experience people, objects, actions and events that are always clear and always the same. These experiences, of people and things that happen in books, are usually, for little children, very real.

- Books are excellent for children's development in all areas, because looking at them can develop concentration and attention span and can lead them into exploring all kinds of language, and, therefore, concepts and ideas. Children learn to imitate, label things and to expand their vocabulary by sharing a book with you. And, apart from anything else, looking at a book together gives you a quiet, cosy time together, and provides you with something to talk about together, thus it encourages development of their conversational skills.

Communication, Language and Literacy

Choosing books

Looking at Books

• • • • • • • • • •

Resources
■ Your book corner (see Related activity)

Learning objective
● To develop an interest in all kinds of books

Preparation
● Work out how you are going to display your books and make them accessible to the children.

What to do
● It is important that you choose the books you are going to offer the children with great care. You should be looking for a wide selection that will suit all the children's levels of development – therefore you will need every kind of book from board books with no text or simple one-word-per-page texts, to books with complex pictures and lots of text.
● Look for books that:
  ◆ raise the children's self-esteem by giving them characters with whom they can identify
  ◆ give opportunities for interaction – eg flap books, pop-up books, books asking questions
  ◆ show real people in a real world
  ◆ reflect the children's interests and experiences
  ◆ show people of all races and cultures and people with disabilities
  ◆ tell about characters who have the same kind of worries and problems as the children.

● Add to these, of course, home-made books that you have made with the children in the group or that they have made at home and brought in.

Extension/variation
● Ask the children to take good care of the books and draw up a set of simple rules together for sharing books.

Links to home
● Ask the parents if the children have any favourite books that they would like to share with the group on a lending basis.

Related activity
● Setting up a book corner (see page 79)

Looking at books together

Any

**All
levels**

Learning objective
● To encourage an interest in books

Preparation
● Try to show the children that you, yourself, enjoy browsing and looking at books, and that books are important to you.

What to do
● Have a looking-at-books session where all the books are out and the idea is to browse. Tell the children that you are all going to spend some time looking at the books, to see what you can see.
● Give them encouragement to choose whichever books they want to look at and give them a comfortable place to sit with their book, or books, and just look at them.
● Some children will find it impossible to browse and choose if they are not used to books at home. Give them as much positive help as you can – say, 'I know a book you would really love – it has great pictures in!' and locate a book that you know will have some interest for that child. Reference books about animals and forms of transport are usually a hit with the boys, who are not always quite so story-orientated as girls.
● At the end of the session, invite individuals to come to the front of the group and talk about their choices.

Extensions/variations
● Encourage children to take books home to share with their parents.
● Give children turns to choose a book for you to read to the group.
● Invite the children to do an illustration of their chosen book. Let them dictate captions for you to write.

Multicultural links
● Obtain some books that are multicultural in illustration and content.
● Get some books in different languages and alphabets so that you can show the children not all books are in English.

Links to home
● Encourage parents to make sharing books with their children an important part of family life.

Resources
■ A broad range of books – board books; pop-up books; storybooks; reference books; picture books, etc
■ Comfortable furnishing, eg floor cushions
■ Paper
■ Drawing implements

Communication, Language and Literacy

© Irene Yates
www.brilliantpublications.co.uk

Read it with feeling

Looking at Books

Resources
- A collection of books, both fiction and nonfiction

Learning objective
- To motivate the children's interest in books

Preparation
- Have your book collection available at all times, where the children can access it easily.

What to do
- Use any occasion that arises to stimulate the children's interest in looking for a book that fits that occasion. You need to know your collection of books fairly well, so that you can immediately say, 'Oh, there's a book about this on the shelf!' and get the children to locate it for you.
- It is much more fun for the children if you read dramatically, emphasizing particular words, or the rhymes or the rhythms that you want the children to respond to. You can pause before you turn a page, encouraging the children to anticipate the next word, or the next action, or picture – all this will bring the text alive for the children and help them to enjoy it more. In many ways, if you use dramatic techniques to translate the text for the children, you will be orchestrating their responses. This is fun for you and for them.

Extensions/variations
- Changing the name of a character to fit a child in the group or someone known to the group.
- Changing the text a little so that it fits the circumstances you are in.
- Staying with a page that is particularly enjoyable, concentrating on the language, the pictures, asking the children for ideas about what is on the page.
- Skipping pages that are less interesting.
- If the text is beyond the children's level, telling it in your own words.

Reading together

Learning objective
- To give children opportunities to behave like readers

Preparation
- Make sure a good selection of books and other material is available and easily accessible to the child.

What to do
- Encourage the child to go through the reading material in order to select something to read with you.
- Choose a peaceful time and a comfortable spot, and be ready to give the reading child your full attention.
- Give the child as much time as she wants to look at the words and the pictures and to respond to them. Encourage her to hold the reading material and turn the pages herself. Wait until it becomes clear that she wants you to read aloud to her.
- Pause for her to fill in the words where she is able and respond by adding in language and reinforcing her knowledge.

Extensions/variations
- Take turns. Give the child plenty of time to say the word or the first part of the word, if she knows it.
- Hold back and reinforce by repeating, when she has got a word right.

Resources
- A collection of all kinds of reading material – books, comics, brochures, etc

Communication, Language and Literacy

Setting up a book corner

Looking at Books

• • • • • • • • • •

Resources
- Table
- Shelves
- Boxes
- Cushions
- Card
- Felt-tip pen
- Library card

Learning objectives
- To present books as meaningful and enjoyable parts of everyday life
- To provide a range of books that support other activities

What to do
- Have a look in your local library and see how the books are made accessible to the children. Usually books for young children are kept at low levels, in boxes with chairs nearby so that the children can easily browse and choose.
- Much will depend upon the space that you have available but aim for a cosy corner where the books can be displayed and the children can sit comfortably to share them with each other and the adults in the setting.
- Choose as large a range of books as possible – make sure that there are picture story books, wordless books, information books, magazines and comics.
- You will probably be able to get a number of books from your local library on long-term loan – and often you can get the librarian to come in and talk to the children about books.

- Explain to the children that all of the books are there for them to share and look at during sessions and you are always happy to see someone 'reading' books, especially if they are reading together.
- At this stage, don't make too much fuss about the books being kept 'tidy' because what you want to do is encourage the children to feel they can handle them freely and look at them whenever they want to.
- Make your display of books look pretty and inviting – you may be able to beg or borrow posters from a local bookshop to enhance your own array of books.
- Make notices saying things like 'The Book Corner is open today' and 'Come and look for a book with your friend'. Read the notices with the children so that they become familiar with them and know what they say.

Class

All levels

Extensions/variations
- Invite parents in to share a period of time at the book corner with some of the children.
- Have a loan system of your own so that the children can choose books to take home.

Related activity
- Library visit (see page 82)

Which book?

 2–3

 All levels

Learning objectives
- To encourage familiarity with books
- To encourage recognition and matching skills
- To encourage vocabulary development and speaking skills

Preparation
- Keep a short time aside for choosing books to look at.

What to do
- Give children turns to choose and pick out a book that they would like the group to share with them.
- Ask them how they know which book they are looking for. They will tell you that they 'recognize' the book – probe them further. Did they recognize the picture on the cover? The pictures inside? Did they recognize the shape and colour of the title? Did they recognize a character? Which other books are about the same character?
- Encourage the child whose turn it is to point to pictures in the book and put them into words, and to connect the pictures with everyday things and events.

Extensions/variations
- Put groups of books together which have a central character, theme or sequence of events and encourage the children to verbalise the differences between them. For example 'This one is about Kipper making a cake, and this one is about Kipper going camping.'
- Bring in new books and ask the children if they can tell what they are about from the illustrations.

Related activity
- Setting up a book corner (see page 79)

Resources
- Your book corner (see Related activity)

© Irene Yates
www.brilliantpublications.co.uk

Book know-how

Looking at Books

● ● ● ● ● ● ● ● ●

Resources
■ A broad range of books

Learning objective
● To familiarize children with books

What to do
● Every time you pick up a book to look at with the children, use book vocabulary, so that the children absorb it naturally. Talk about 'the cover', 'the pages', 'the illustrations'.

● Try and engender in them a love of books, which is easily done if you are yourself enthusiastic about books.

● Share your reading with them – talking about 'words', 'sentences' and 'letters' and encouraging them to predict what might happen next, what the next word might be, etc.

● Ask them to show you things such as:
  ◆ the first page
  ◆ the last page
  ◆ the top of the page
  ◆ the bottom of the page
  ◆ the front of the book
  ◆ the back of the book
  ◆ the beginning of the story
  ◆ a word
  ◆ a line
  ◆ a caption – the words under the picture
  ◆ the word that comes next
  ◆ the page numbers
  ◆ the title
  ◆ the author's name.

Extension/variation
● Turn the 'showing' around – show *them* the top of the page, etc, and ask them what it is.

Multicultural links
● Try to get hold of some books in other languages so that you can show that not all writing reads in the same direction and not all alphabets look the same.

Related activity
● Book words (see page 167)

Any

Library visit

Learning objectives
- To encourage a love of books
- To raise awareness of library provision in the locality

Preparation
- Try to arrange a pre-visit with the librarian to find out what is on offer. Librarians are only too happy to get children hooked on books right from the beginning and will often suggest running a story time, lending extra books, making a regular visit to the group, etc. It would be particularly helpful if each child could choose a book to borrow.
- You can either take the group as a whole, or do several trips with smaller groups.

What to do
- Discuss the impending visit with the children so that they know what is expected of them. Make the visit as much fun as possible.
- Afterwards, allow the children to discuss the trip on their own terms. Make time to share the borrowed books and talk about them.
- Invite the children to talk about their chosen book to the rest of the group.

Extension/variation
- Arrange follow-up trips.

Links to home
- Ask for parent helpers for the visit.
- Encourage parents to visit the library with the children and to take out a library ticket for them.

Resources
- Local library or library van

 Ensure correct child : adult ratio for visit.

Communication, Language and Literacy

© Irene Yates
www.brilliantpublications.co.uk

Reading Moments

Looking at Books

• • • • • • • • • •

Resources

- Lots of books of all kinds and other reading material (magazines, comics, brochures, etc)

Learning objective

- To encourage an interest in books

Preparation

- Make sure there are lots of books accessible at all times.

What to do

- Children sometimes get the impression that books and reading are only for specific times and places – ie story telling time at the group! Unless they are surrounded by reading material at home and have a reading family, the activity does not appear to them to be a natural one!
- Introduce Reading Moments to them. Any moment can be a Reading Moment. When you have finished one activity and aren't quite ready to go on to another one, why not settle down for five minutes with a book? Reading Moments can happen inside or outside, they can be short moments or long moments, they can be sharing moments or solitary moments, they can be profound thinking moments or having-a-laugh moments. Try to get this concept across to the children by demonstrating that you, too, have Reading Moments, and that you enjoy them very much.
- Give lots of positive feedback.

Extensions/variations

- You may have to have one or two simple rules – for example, if someone has a Reading Moment outside, they always bring the book back in before they go on to something else.
- Try to keep Reading Moments as informal as possible. If the children want to talk about what they have read, encourage them, but don't discuss their reading as a matter of course because it will seem to them as though every Reading Moment is followed by a Big Interrogation Moment!

Links to home

- Explain the Reading Moments concept to parents and encourage them to have reading matter available to follow the strategy at home.

Related activity

- Sharing a book (see page 84)

Sharing a book

• • • • • • • • • •

Class

Learning objective
● To stimulate interest in books

Preparation
● Choose a book with a repetitive pattern, such as *Brown Bear, Brown Bear, What Do You See?* Read the book to the children and show them the pictures.

What to do
● At the top of each page of your paper, print a part of the story. Read it with the children, tracking each word as you go, and encouraging them to join in.
● Give the children a small piece of paper to illustrate a part of the story. Stick their pictures to the appropriate pages – get them to help you decide which of your pages each illustration belongs to. It doesn't matter how many versions of an illustration you stick to each of your large pages as long as the children all contribute to as many as they can.
● Put card at the front and back of your pages, punch holes and use the rings to hold it together.
● Read through the book together, tracking the words. Read the original book with the children again and invite them to make comparisons.

Extensions/variations
● Do this with any of the children's favourites.
● Put the group books in the book corner with 'real' books.
● Invite the children to read and share the books whenever they have a 'Reading Moment'.

Links to home
● Encourage the children to take the books home to share with their families.

Related activity
● Reading Moments (see page 83)

Resources
■ *Brown Bear, Brown Bear, What Do You See?* by Bill Martin and Eric Carle (Picture Lions) or alternative books with strong repetitive pattern
■ Sheets of paper 30cm x 45cm
■ Black felt pen
■ Smaller pieces of paper
■ Glue
■ 2 pieces of card 30cm x 45cm
■ Hole punch
■ Binder rings

© Irene Yates
www.brilliantpublications.co.uk

Towards Reading

- Our literate society is abuzz with written symbols. We see them every time we move, every time we walk down the street or enter and leave a building. Our aim, at the Foundation Stage, should be to inspire our children with the confidence that they are able to become a part of that literate society.

- That is not to say that we want to be teaching them, formally, to read and write, but that we want to open the doors for them that will allow them to learn to read and write when they are ready.

- The opportunities that we make for them to understand symbols and to know that print carries meaning make them aware of print and lead them to the gradual recognition and identification of symbols and, thus, of print.

- There is probably no task or activity that could not, if a little imagination is used, carry an opportunity for reading and writing.

- Probably the most important thing we can do for our future readers is to show them that we are readers, that we enjoy the activity and get lots out of it, and that we believe they can be readers too.

- There is much to say for encouraging children to read along with us before they can actually 'read'. Help them to track the direction of the print and to notice which sounds begin and end words, before you even start giving them the names of letters.

- Children enjoy playing with sounds; they love playing games such as I-Spy, or finding out how many words they can say that begin with a specific sound, or finding out how many new words they can make by changing a sound in the middle of the word (eg <u>bit</u>, <u>bat</u>, <u>but</u>).

www.brilliantpublications.co.uk

Communication, Language and Literacy

- If you read a story with the page facing towards the children, and track your finger along the line they will often recognize the first sound, and then identify the word that they predict. Prediction skills are an essential part of learning to read; much of the children's language development will help them to predict (or guess) which word is coming next, or which word *might* come next, and you can give them lots of praise and encouragement for their prediction being right.

- They also love playing matching games and it is a short step from matching pairs of pictures (snake to snake) to matching a sound symbol and a picture ('s' to snake), and, from there, to matching word to picture (*snake* to snake). Along with knowing the direction that the print is moving in and that the gaps between words are there for a reason, they are well on the way to reading.

- The activities in this section are designed to give the children lots of experience but not too much formal 'reading and writing' work. Games are easily the most enjoyable ways to learn and the more fun you make them, the better.

- You don't need lots of expensive commercially produced material – it takes a bit of thought and a little time to produce your own equipment, but it has an added value for the children in that you have taken the time and trouble to make it for *them*, so it has to be good!

© Irene Yates
www.brilliantpublications.co.uk

Be a reading role model

Towards Reading

. . . .

Resources
- Brochures
- Maps
- Timetables
- Directories
- Recipe cards
- Magazines
- Comics
- Labels
- Notices, etc

Learning objectives
- To show children that reading is a normal part of everyday life
- To introduce children to a range of different reading materials

What to do
- It is easy to get hung up on the idea of 'books' being the only reading material you need to offer the group. However, to present a good reading environment you want the children to feel comfortable with all kinds of material.
- Start a collection of all kinds of different material. You can get freebies from lots of different places – shops, stations, information centres – and all of the material will help to make the children aware that reading is not just something that happens in books.
- Use the material, for them to see, whenever you can. For example, if you are going to watch a TV programme, let them help you to look up the programme in the TV guide; if you are making a visit, show them how to locate your destination on a map. You are not aiming at this time to get your children to 'read', but merely to observe how useful reading is in your daily life.

- Make as much use of notes and lists as you can and encourage the children to help you to plan events and outings, using information packs to help you.

Extension/variation
- Make regular trips to the library or the library bus and help the children to understand how the books are sorted.

Links to home
- Ask parents to encourage children to bring leaflets and maps to 'show and tell' when they have been on family trips or events.

Related activity
- Sharing books (see page 91)

Look for words

Learning objective

● To begin to recognize some familiar words

Preparation

● Look for spaces and situations that you can easily write words, captions and labels for.

What to do

● Make one of the points of your caption-and label-writing that the children see you do it, read it with you, and understand why it is there.

● For instance, you may want to ask the children to keep the books tidy. Discuss this in circle time, and suggest to the children that you write a label together to remind them. What should your label say? When you have come to an agreement, demonstrate writing it, read it through together, pointing to the words as you read, and decide together where the label should be placed.

● When you are by the books ask the children to tell you what the label says. Can they point out any of the words? For instance, you may ask, 'Which word says 'book'?' and reinforce the beginning sound and letter to help them.

Extensions/variations

● Help the children to write labels and captions for their play situations, eg in the post office write 'Stamps' and 'Queue here', or other phrases that the children want, and regularly ask them to read the words back to you.

● Write familiar words for other areas that you are exploring, draw the children's attention to them and 'read' them together frequently.

Resources
■ Card
■ Felt-tip pens

© Irene Yates
www.brilliantpublications.co.uk

Making stories

Resources
- Approximately five objects, such as a toy, a birthday card, a picture, an item of clothing
- Paper
- Writing and drawing implements

Learning objectives
- To give opportunities for creating stories
- To give opportunities to interact with others to make up a story

Preparation
- Make a collection of objects – you could collect these by asking various children to choose something to bring for the story. The children need to be sitting quietly, as for circle time.

What to do
- Explain to the children that you are going to make up a story together. Show the children the collection of objects you have made. The idea is to make up a story that has as many of the things in it as possible. The story has to make as much sense as possible, also.
- Before you start, ask, 'Who will our story be about?' You might find that the children want to stick to known characters to begin with, until they have the idea, but that's fine, they can be more adventurous later!
- Go round the circle asking each child to make a contribution to the story. Keep the objects on view so that the children can remember what they are, and they will act as a stimulant to the development of the story.

Extension/variation
- If the children are excited by the story they have made up, get some of them to help you make a book of it, with them doing the pictures and verbalizing the words, which you then demonstrate writing.

Reading together

1–3

All levels

Learning objectives
- To develop good responses to books
- To develop a love of books
- To develop awareness of how print works

Preparation
- Have lots of books and print material to hand.

What to do
- Encourage the child to choose a book for you to read together. If it is a story that the child is unfamiliar with, read it to her first. Then suggest, 'Shall we read it together?'
- Have the child/children close so that you are giving the activity a feeling of cosiness. Let the child do as much as possible to interpret the pictures and the words, prompt where appropriate, and take over where appropriate.
- Work together through the text; point with your finger to match the words to the spoken language.

Extension/variation
- Encourage the child to choose a book completely new to her, look through it together first, helping her to anticipate what it might be about, then read it to her.

Resources
- All kinds of books and print material

Communication, Language and Literacy

Sharing books

Towards Reading

• • • • • • • • • •

Resources
■ Lots of books and other print materials

Learning objectives
● To develop a love of books
● To develop early reading skills

Preparation
● Make 'sharing a story' a very important and enjoyable time, if you can have a specific time each day – for example, after juice and biscuits – it will help the children to anticipate it.

What to do
● Good reading habits that last a lifetime come from making children's first introduction to books and stories as enjoyable as possible. Early reading skills are absorbed when we:
   ◆ Make sure the child can see both the print and the pictures
   ◆ Point to the words as we read them, showing the left to right direction
   ◆ Use the pictures, which may have a second 'story' in them
   ◆ Pause occasionally – ask, 'What do you think is going to happen next?'
   ◆ Leave space for discussion where appropriate, before turning the page
   ◆ Encourage the children to 'read' or retell the story to us
   ◆ Go back time and time again to favourite stories.

● Let the children choose the books that they want you to share and ask them, 'What is it about?' 'What do you like about it?' 'Who is the character?' 'What does the character do?' 'Is it a good ending?' 'Why?' etc.
● Encourage the children to join in with the words, or take over the reading from you, whenever they can.

Extension/variation
● Demonstrate to parents how to share books enjoyably with children, and encourage them to imitate your role at home.

© Irene Yates
www.brilliantpublications.co.uk

Communication, Language and Literacy

Whole words

• • • • • • • • •

Learning objective
● To look for and observe words which are seen frequently in the environment

Preparation
● Talk to the children about the words that we see around us every day and alert them to be observant in spotting them.

What to do
● Discuss the words that you see close to your setting, or in your setting. For example the words 'Push', 'Pull', 'Exit', 'Fire Door' may be around you on the walls and doors.
● Children are also used to seeing their own names and their friends' names in the setting. Encourage them to observe the words – they will soon begin to note, or absorb, the shape and the pattern that the print makes for each word. Encourage them to remember and recognize the words – this is the beginning of reading.
● Make a collection of the words the children recall seeing, perhaps in the street or the park.

Extensions/variations
● Make a display of the words and draw attention to them when appropriate.
● All areas can be drawn into this step into literacy – look for numbers in the street, look for words in the park, the local shops, etc.

Resources
■ Card
■ Felt-tip pens

Communication, Language and Literacy

I can...

Towards Reading

• • • • • • • • • •

Resources

■ No special requirements

Learning objectives
● To give opportunities for understanding, recognizing and identifying initial sounds
● To introduce the idea of the alphabet and alphabetical order

What to do
● This is a game that can be played over and over again. The children take turns, in order. Ask the first child to tell something that she can do beginning with 'a' – for example, *ask*. The next child thinks of something she can do beginning with 'b' – for example, *bite*. Keep going throughout the alphabet. You might have to leave some letters out if they prove too difficult (or make up some silly words!). If you have been through the alphabet once and have started again, you can't accept the same words.

Extensions/variations
● Change the theme so that, for example, instead of thinking of something they can *do*, the children think of something they can eat or drink, or something they can see.
● Sing the alphabet song.

Match the letter

Learning objectives

- To provide opportunities for identifying and matching letters
- To develop an awareness of alphabetical order

Preparation

- Photocopy the Match the letter templates (pages 176–178) on to thin card. Cut into cards. Cover with sticky-back plastic (optional).

What to do

- Write a letter on the flip chart or board. Ask the children which sound it is. Give the children turns to find the matching letter in the alphabet bank. If the children have an alphabet bank each, ask them all to find the letter; the first to find it gets a point.

Extensions/variations

- When the children know all their letter sounds, make capital letter cards and play the game with them.
- Look for letters that begin or end words that you are familiarizing the children with during other activities.

Related activity

- Forming letters (see page 179)

Resources

- Match the letter templates on pages 176–178
- Thin card
- Scissors
- Sticky-back plastic (optional)
- Felt-tip pen
- Flip chart or easel or board

Communication, Language and Literacy

© Irene Yates
www.brilliantpublications.co.uk

Misfit words

Towards Reading

• • • • • • • • •

Resources
■ No special requirements

Learning objective
● To give opportunities for auditory discrimination

Preparation
● This activity will encourage the children to observe how sounds are not just one mass of sound, but have great differences.

What to do
● Explain to the children that you are going to give them groups of words; they must listen carefully and put up their hands to tell you which word in the group begins with a different sound from the others. Call out a series of words that begin with the same initial sound, including one word that begins with something different – for example: *bag*, *bed*, *ball*, *chair*, *banana*.

Extension/variation
● Ask the children to become leaders – they need to give at least three words beginning with the same sound and one with a different one. At first, they will probably always leave the misfit till the end. Try to encourage them to think about this before they decide on their words.

"bear, bean, cabbage!"

Right order

Learning objectives
- To develop sequencing skills
- To give opportunities for retelling a narrative

Preparation
- Using a storybook that the children have shared with you, draw and colour simple pictures of the main events, one to each piece of card, and mix them up.

What to do
- Tell the children you have done some pictures of the story they liked but now you've finished them you need their help in getting them in the right order.
- Put all the pictures down on a flat surface, in any order, and ask the children to look at them and tell you what they can see. If you don't tell them what the story is, you will give them the added interest of trying to 'guess'.
- Encourage the children to look at each picture and describe in words what they think is happening in it. Let them do as much of the talking as possible, between them, and only intervene if they get really stuck.
- Their next task is to lay the pictures in the order in which the story happened – encourage them to use time and sequencing words and phrases, such as 'in the beginning', 'at the start', 'to begin with', 'and then', 'next', 'last of all', 'this is how it ended'.

- When the pictures are in the right order, get the children to 'read' and retell the story to you.

Extensions/variations
- Use stories with a repetitive refrain. When the children decide that the refrain needs to be in the sequence, write the words for them on more pieces of card and invite the children to place them in the correct places between the pictures.
- Help them to 'read' the words.

Related activity
- Order, order (see page 100)

Resources
- Paper or card
- Felt-tip pens

Communication, Language and Literacy

© Irene Yates
www.brilliantpublications.co.uk

Same and different

● ● ● ● ● ● ● ● ● ●

Resources
- Same and different template on page 174
- Sticky-back plastic (optional)
- Paper
- Card
- Felt-tip pens
- Scissors

Learning objective
● To observe differences and similarities

Preparation
● One of the most important skills for reading development is to recognize things that are the same and things that are different.
● Photocopy the Same and different template on page 174. Cut out the cards. Covering them with sticky-back plastic will prolong their use.
● You could photocopy or use the computer copy facility to reproduce an image to make your own 'Same and different' cards.

What to do
● Talk about the sets of cards. Ask the children to look for *what's the same* and *what's different*. Encourage them to verbalize and describe the differences and similarities.
● Play games with the cards:
    ◆ Put all the cards face up on the table and ask the child/children to collect all the cards which match each other.
    ◆ Put all the cards face up on the table and ask the child/children to collect all the cards which don't match any others.
    ◆ Put all the cards face down on the table and turn them over in turns, trying to make matching pairs.
    ◆ Put all the cards face down on the table and turn them over in turns, discarding the matches and trying to 'catch' all the ones that don't match any others.

Extension/variation
● Make cards with letters or familiar words for very able children and play the same games.

1-4

Sound box

Learning objective

- To familiarize children with letter sounds

Preparation

- Make a set of labels of initial sounds that you want the children to learn. For each letter sound, cut and stick, or draw, a picture of something the children will recognize. For example for 'b' cut and stick a picture of a bear, as a cue.

What to do

- Have the children sitting in a circle and show them the box. Identify the picture and the sound. Have a short session of thinking of things or words that begin with that sound.
- The game is for the children to take turns to look around the room and locate something that begins with the sound. They fetch the object and show it to the group, who agree or disagree. If the group agrees, the object goes into the box.
- At the end of the game, take out the items one by one, identifying them and their initial sound, and return them to their original

Extensions/variations

- Have three sound boxes on the go at the same time and let the children choose which sound they will try for.
- Invite the children to bring in things from home for the collections, on specific days.

Resources

- Large cardboard box
- Card for labels
- Felt-tip pens
- Magazines (for pictures)
- Scissors
- Glue

Communication, Language and Literacy

© Irene Yates
www.brilliantpublications.co.uk

Making labels

Towards Reading

• • • • • • • • • •

Resources
■ Computer
■ Word processing program
■ Printer
■ Paper or thin card (white or light colours)
■ Scissors
■ Reusable mastic adhesive

Learning objectives
● To familiarize the children with the computer
● To make labels and captions

What to do
● Suggest to the children that you could put labels on some of the equipment, or places, in the group base. Suggest that it would be a good idea to do them together on the computer.
● Decide on your labels. You might want to just put 'Crayons', for example, or you might want to put something like 'Be gentle with the guinea pig'.
● Choose a large, clear font that the children can discriminate easily.
● Ask them, 'Which sound comes first? So that is letter ….' Talk them though the whole activity. Help the children to type the letters in by showing you how to locate them on the keyboard.
● Help the children to save and print.
● Cut out the labels and stick them where the children want them to be.

Extensions/variations
● You can make this quite a regular activity because labels and captions tend to get tatty very quickly. Help the children to see that, if you tidy them up by making new ones every so often, you keep your base nice and tidy.
● Be prepared to change the wording if someone comes up with a better idea. Again, make new labels.

Links to home
● Make labels for the children to take home, eg 'Mia's bedroom', 'Atak's rabbit'.

Order, order

(3–5)

Learning objective
- To develop sequencing skills

Preparation
- Photocopy the Order, order template on page 175 on to thin card. Colour in with felt-tip pens. Cut the sheet up into separate cards. Covering the cards with sticky-back plastic will make them last longer.

What to do
- Mix up the cards of each set. (Don't mix the sets together!)
- Look at the cards with the children, asking them what they can see. Suggest that if the cards were in the right order they would 'tell a story'.
- Ask the children to put them into the right order and 'read' the story to you.

Extensions/variations
- For children who are really good at sequencing, cut story strips out of comics. Get them to work in pairs to put the story into the right order and 'read' it to you.
- Make up your own sequencing cards.

Related activity
- Right order (see page 96)

Resources
- Order, order template on page 175
- Thin card
- Felt-tip pens
- Scissors
- Sticky-back plastic (optional)

Communication, Language and Literacy

Pocket letters

Towards Reading

Resources
- Card
- Sticky tape
- Scissors
- Felt-tip pens

Learning objective
- To familiarize children with letters and sounds

Preparation
- Make a display out of the card, giving it 26 pockets. Make these pockets look like little beds. Mark each bed with a letter of the alphabet (lower case). Make 26 small cards which will fit into the pockets, mark each one with a letter of the alphabet (lower case).

What to do
- Show the children the display. Talk about the alphabet and letter sounds, to familiarize them with this vocabulary. Remember not to add the 'uh' when you are making the sounds of letters.
- Show the children the cards. Suggest that they take turns to put a card to bed in its appropriate pocket.
- Hold up each card, ask the children what sound they think it says and choose a child to match it with its 'bed' and place it in the pocket.

Extensions/variations
- When the children are familiar with single letters, make 'beds' for double and cluster sounds, such as 'ch', 'br', 'st', 'str'.
- Develop this strategy by using whole words instead of letters, using children's name cards, or other key words that they are familiar with. These can be words from their favourite books or the names of things that have labels in your setting, or weather, or dinosaurs, or any other words you think the children will know.

Class

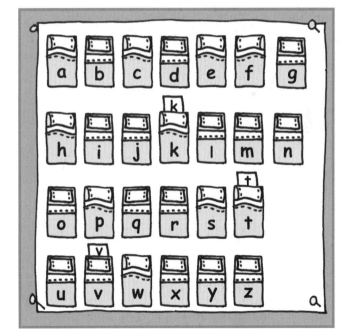

What I liked was...

Learning objective
- To show an understanding of the elements of stories

Preparation
- Read your book and have some ideas about what you would like to say about it.

What to do
- Look at the book with the children and discuss the features that they can see – the title, the author, the illustrations, etc. If there is a blurb on the back, read the blurb out to them. Tell them that you have read the book and really enjoyed it and tell them the main characters, the main events, how it began and how it ended. Tell them why you liked it – perhaps it had a good repeating pattern, or it was funny, or it reminded you of something in your life.
- Tell the children that you would like them to tell the group about a book that they have enjoyed, in the way that you have told them – talking about the characters and the main things that happen. Ask them to choose a book and tell the group something about it.
- Record the children's reviews onto the cassette tape and play them back to them.

Extension/variation
- Get the children to dictate their ideas to you or another adult. Write them down, get the children to illustrate them, and make a 'Book Review' display.

Resources
- A storybook you know
- Tape recorder
- Blank cassette tape
- Paper and writing implements (to make own book)

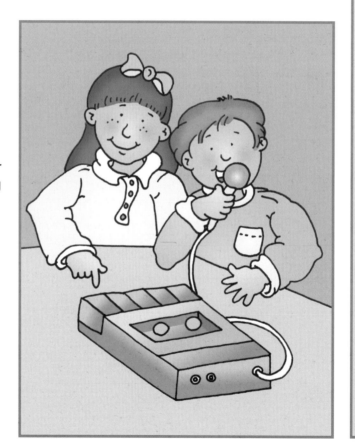

© Irene Yates
www.brilliantpublications.co.uk

Silly sentences

Towards Reading

• • • • • • • • • •

Resources
■ Paper
■ Felt-tip pen

Learning objectives
● To hear and say initial sounds in words
● To link sounds to letters
● To develop an awareness of alliteration

Preparation
● Have the children sitting together, ready to concentrate.

What to do
● Tell the children the rhyme 'Peter Piper pecked…' (see page 184).
● Ask them if they think you could all make up some silly sentences together. Invite them to choose a sound that they would like to have a go with to begin. Write the letter sound on one of the pieces of paper and show it to the children. Say the sound, and ask them to say it back to you. Make sure they do not add the 'uh' sound.
● Ask the children if they can think up a silly sentence. Give them a simple one to start with – for example, for the 's' sound, *Sam said sausages*, or *Sardines sing silly songs*, etc.
● Play this game in any odd minutes, ideally covering all the letter sounds over a period of time.

Extensions/variations
● Write out the silly sentences and ask the children to illustrate them for a display.
● Go on to double consonants and consonant clusters when you feel it will work. For example:
   ◆ *Pretty princesses have no prickles.*
   ◆ *Clever clocks clatter.*
   ◆ *Straight streets stretch.*

Colour words

Learning objectives
- To hear and say initial sounds
- To write simple words

Preparation
- Use coloured sheets of sugar paper to make a book. Put the sheets together, punch two holes down one side and secure with ring clips. On white A4 write the title 'Our Colour Book', draw a bubble round it in a chosen colour, cut out and stick to front cover.
- Get the children to sit, ready to listen and join in.

What to do
- Discuss the colours of the pages.
- Ask the children to tell you the sound each colour begins with. Finger-trace the letters of the sounds in the air.
- Write the letters and then the words on a flip chart.
- Give each child a sheet of white paper. Ask them to select a colour. Help them to trace, copy or write the sound their colour begins with on their paper. Draw a bubble round it, cut out and stick to the appropriate page.

Extensions/variations
- Depending on the stages the children have reached, they can trace, copy or write whole words.
- Select and cut out coloured pictures or text to add to relevant pages.

Resources
- Sugar paper (different colours)
- Hole punch
- Ring clips
- White A4 paper
- Coloured felt-tip pens
- Glue-stick
- Flip chart

Communication, Language and Literacy

Shopping trip

• • • • • • • • • •

Resources
- Grocery packets
- Scissors
- Card
- Glue
- Shopping bags
- Large box

Learning objectives
- To know that print carries meaning
- To read a range of familiar and common words independently

Preparation
- Find two of each item of grocery, eg cereal packets, toothpaste packets, tissue boxes, milk powder cans, etc. Cut the label from one packet and put the other packet in the large box or set them up in your shopping corner. Glue the cut out labels to pieces of card to make them more sturdy.

What to do
- Give each child a shopping bag. Share out the labels between them. Tell the children that the labels which they have are their own shopping list. What you want them to do is go to the shop, or box, and find the items which they have labels for.
- When they bring back their shopping in the bags, ask them to sort out each packet and match it to its label. Can the children 'read' the labels and packets to you?

Extension/variation
- Play a shopping game with all the children. Have them sitting in a circle and the packets on display somewhere in the room. Hold out the labels, upside down so that the children don't know what they are. Give each child a turn to take a label, turn it over, then locate the right packet and bring it back to the circle. Give stickers for getting it right, and stickers for being able to 'read' the packet.

Print walk

Learning objective
- To provide opportunities to look for environmental print

Preparation
- Have the children ready to go for a walk.

What to do
- Tell the children that you are going out for a walk and that it is a special kind of walk because you are going to look for all the things you can see that have words printed – in other words, *writing*.
- Encourage the children to look for road signs, road names, shop names, house names, notices in shop windows, advertisements, billboards, etc.
- Every time they see one, give them praise and help them to 'read' it, encouraging them to give you any of the sounds that they can see. Read the word/s then ask them to repeat them to you and read them again together.
- When you get back to your setting, talk about all the print that you saw, ask the children what they can remember and make a list of it for them on the flip chart, which you can then 'read' back together.

Extensions/variations
- Make a set of road signs, road names and shop names and build up a small locality for role play activities.
- Look for specific street print – for instance, if you are doing a project on 'water', look for a 'Swimming Pool' sign or a 'No swimming in the lake' sign, etc.

Links to home
- Ask for parent helpers to go on the walk.

Resources
- Your setting
- Large sheet of paper on flip chart or easel
- Felt-tip pen

 Ensure correct adult : child ratios.

Naming names

Towards Reading

• • • • • • • • • •

Resources
■ Cards with children's names written on (see page 108)

Learning objective
● To recognize whole words/names

Preparation
● Make sure the children have had the chance to familiarize themselves with the name cards of everyone in the group.

What to do
● Tell the children that they are going to play a name game, called 'Naming names'. Take the cards with the group's names on, put them face up on a table or flat surface. Ask the children, in turns, to find the card with their own name on and pick it up. (It is interesting to see which children can still recognize their name even if the letters aren't the right way up to where they're sitting.)
● When all the cards are collected, take them back and mix them up. Put them out on the table again. Give a child's name, and ask for someone else to find it. The child whose name it is can look but not touch or show where it is – until the other children have had a chance to recognize and take it.

Extensions/variations
● Play the same game with different words – eg words the children are fairly familiar with from their books, videos or from environmental print.
● Use words familiar to the children, appropriate to other key areas, for example in maths you might use the names of specific shapes.

Related activity
● Know-a-name (see page 108)

Know-a-name

(4–6)

Learning objective
● To familiarize children with their own name and others' names

Preparation
● Make sure all the children know each other's names. Make a card with each child's name on and for all the adult helpers.

What to do
● Hold up one card at a time. Ask the children whose name it is. Hopefully, the child whose name it is will recognize it, if not, give clues, such as '…it begins with the sound of…'. When making the sounds, give a clear sound without an 'uh' ending – for instance say 'sssss' not 'suh'.
● Give each card to the appropriate child. Give them lots of opportunity to share their cards with each other, showing, talking, comparing and contrasting. For example, you can say things like, 'Whose name has got a 'h' sound in it?' etc.
● Collect the cards in for another time.

Extensions/variations
● Make sure that all the adults in the group have a name card as well, and share them with the children.
● Play a game where you give a child a name and they have to give it to the child whose name it is.
● Encourage the children to write their own names and notice others' names on all of their pieces of work.

Related activity
● Naming names (see page 107)

Resources
■ Small pieces of card
■ Felt-tip pen

Communication, Language and Literacy

Matching shapes

Resources
- Coloured card
- Scissors

Learning objective
- To give opportunities for visual discrimination

Preparation
- This activity will encourage the children to notice how all the shapes in a set are actually different from each other, which will lead them to observe how letters and words differ from one another.
- Cut out shapes of various sizes, squares, rectangles, circles and triangles.

What to do
- Mix up all the shapes. Ask the children to sort the pieces of card into sets according to shape only. Encourage the children to discuss the idea of 'same' and 'different'. Talk about the colours and sizes and ask the children to describe to you what is different about the shapes.

Extension/variation
- Encourage the children to invent games with the shapes, so that they might have all the triangles together but laid out in size order, biggest first or smallest first – or lay them in sets of colours.

What does he like?

Any

Learning objective
● To provide opportunities for initial sounds work

Preparation
● Make sure the children all know the name of the puppet or toy.

What to do
● Have the children sitting comfortably together, in a circle. Begin by introducing the puppet. For example: 'This is Ben the Bear. He likes things that begin with the sound of his name. So he likes things that begin with 'b'.' Avoid saying 'buh'. Ask the children to go round the circle, thinking of things that begin with the relevant sound.

● To begin with, the children will think only of nouns – for example, *bubbles, bath, biscuit*. Lead them to think of things that Ben (or whoever) might like *doing* – ie verbs – as well. For example, *bouncing, baking, building*. Then think of things that Ben might be *like* – ie adjectives, such as *beautiful, bright, bumpy*.

Extension/variation
● Play a memory game where the children have to *add on* the things that Ben likes. For example, first person says *bubbles*, second person says *bubbles and baths*, third person says *bubbles and baths and biscuits*. How far can the children get before they are in a muddle?

Resources
■ A puppet or toy

Communication, Language and Literacy

Letter train

Resources

- Letter train template on page 173
- Felt-tip pens
- Sticky-back plastic or laminator (optional)
- Die
- Counters

Learning objectives

- To name and sound letters of the alphabet
- To absorb order of alphabet

Preparation

- Enlarge the Letter train template on page 173 to A3 size. Photocopy on to thin card. Colour in if you wish. Laminating or covering with sticky-back plastic will make the game board last longer.
- Children need to be at a steady table or in an isolated place on the floor.

What to do

- Give each child a counter. Instruct them to take turns to throw a die. They move their counter the number of coaches that they throw, saying the sound that they land on. If they can't say the sound the others must tell them and they repeat it. They must get the right number to land on 'z' to finish the game. First there wins.

Extensions/variations

- More able children could be asked to give up to three words beginning, or ending, with the sound they land on.
- Make another board with capital letters, and children say names of the letters.

Enjoying Stories

- In order to become people who read, we need children to enjoy stories right from the very beginning. This means getting the conditions right, from the start.

- All children enjoy the close-up feel of sitting with someone either telling or reading a story to them. They like the intimacy and the shared imagination, the warmth and feeling comfortable.

- When they really begin to listen, they like the way storytellers play with words, they enjoy the challenge of new language and new language patterns, and they like to think that they can anticipate what comes next.

- Frequent listening means that children soon begin to understand what *makes* a story, and how stories work. Stories provide an exciting way into new worlds and new situations and, even though there may be danger in the story, the child is still safe whilst living the story vicariously.

- The activities in this section are designed to stimulate a response to stories – that response may be manifested in many different ways. Stories that help our children to reflect upon their feelings and the feelings of others are an important part of their development. So are stories that become favourites – a child may want the same story over and over again for a long time because it satisfies some urge or feeling inside her and then she may move on to something new, or not, as the case may be. We can all remember stories that seemed to be an important part of our childhood, even though we probably couldn't say why. The truth is that when we identify with the character, or characters, we are living out something of importance in our own lives and perhaps this is why these stories seem to stay with us for ever.

- A child who enjoys hearing and listening to stories is a child who will be curious to learn to read, who will want to do it because it is 'a satisfying activity' – a child who is intrinsically motivated.

© Irene Yates
www.brilliantpublications.co.uk

Huff, puff

● ● ● ● ● ● ● ● ●

Resources

■ The story of *The Three Little Pigs* (for story line see page 189)
■ Three lightweight pieces of fabric (eg chiffon scarves)
■ Space for children to sit and listen, and move

Learning objectives

● To give opportunities to share and enjoy a story
● To give opportunities to link language with physical movement

Preparation

● Read or tell the story of *The Three Little Pigs* to the children. Emphasise the chorus of 'I'll huff and I'll puff and I'll blow your house down!' Practise huffing and puffing.

What to do

● Group the children into three teams, sitting in lines, one child behind the other. Tell the children that they are going to play the 'Huffing and Puffing' game. The chorus this time is, 'I'll huff and I'll puff and I'll blow your scarf away'.
● The first child in each team stands and holds a scarf. They have to let go of the scarf and huff and puff to see how far they can make it travel. When the scarf drops they sit down at the spot the scarf has reached. The next child in the team takes the scarf and starts from there.
● Continue until all the children are sitting down. To finish the session, ask the children to retell the story.

Extensions/variations

● You can play with balloons but they are harder to control!
● Play with just a small group and let them all have a scarf.
● Make the game competitive by seeing which team finishes first, or who moves the furthest.

Act-a-story – Goldilocks

Learning objective
- To give opportunities to reflect on and recount stories

Preparation
- You will need to be familiar with the story of *Goldilocks and the Three Bears*. With the card, draw and cut out three bowls, three chairs and three beds. You could also make some trees to be the wood, and a little cottage.

What to do
- Choose children to hold the cards. Choose someone to be Goldilocks, and three children to be the three bears. With the help of all the children, check that the children who have the parts know what they have to say when you reach the repetitive bits of speech.
- Begin to tell the story. Have the children with the cottage and the wood hold up their pictures for the first part.
- Introduce the three bears with their three bowls. Encourage them to join in. You say, 'The first bear was...' and the child says '...a great big bear'; you say, 'The second bear was...' and the child says '...a middle-sized bear', etc. Encourage the children to use a 'great big' voice, a 'middle-sized' voice and a 'small, wee' voice throughout the story by saying, for example, 'The first bear said in his great big voice...'.

Extension/variation
- Retell the story as many times as necessary for everyone to have a turn at being part of the acting out.
- Encourage the children to act out, or improvize, the story without supervision.

Resources
- Story line for *Goldilocks and the Three Bears* (see page 187)
- Card
- Scissors
- Felt-tip pen

Communication, Language and Literacy

The Three Billy Goats Gruff

Enjoying Stories

• • • • • • • • • •

Resources
■ A version of *The Three Billy Goats Gruff* (see page 189)

Learning objectives
● To give opportunities for sharing and enjoying a story
● To give opportunities for predicting outcomes/words/phrases

Preparation
● If this is the first time you have introduced the story, first read it to the children, showing them the illustrations.

What to do
● Go back to the beginning of the story, telling the children that this time you are all going to tell the story together.
● Begin by making a silly mistake, like saying, 'Once upon a time there were three billy goats gruff all in the shopping centre…' so that the children can correct you.
● Add little bits of the story at a time but get the children to fill in the main information, just by pausing at the right moment. For example, 'The three billy goats were eating the…?'
● What you are after is the children listening intently so that they can anticipate what is going to come next and join in.

Extensions/variations
● Use the same strategy when reading or reciting rhymes, so that the children can anticipate the rhyming patterns and the rhyming words.

Be a storyteller

Any

All
levels

Learning objective

- To add to the enjoyment of listening to stories

Preparation

- Read the story in a picture book several times, until you have grasped the main characters, events and bits of repetitive language. Rehearse it in your mind before you tell it. Be prepared to adapt and shorten or lengthen the story to suit the children's attention and their enthusiasm to participate. Try to find some 'props' that will help you to tell the story. For instance: puppets or finger puppets; cut-out pictures; any object that acts as a visual aid for you and for the children.

What to do

- *Telling* the story, rather than *reading* it, gives you the opportunity to be spontaneous about where and when you offer it. As you're telling the story, you can watch to see how the children are responding, who is participating and who is not, how enthusiastic they are, and how much attention they are displaying.
- Think ahead about specific actions and intonations that you can use. Leave pauses where the repetitive words and phrases come in, so that the children can anticipate what's coming next. Make it interesting and fun, using all your powers to dramatize and emphasize the rhythm of the story and the words you want the children to pick up.
- Their response will tell you how well you are doing!

Extension/variation

- There's a place for both telling and reading and, don't forget, *making up your own stories*!

Related activity

- Making puppets (see page 119)

Resources

- Whichever stories or books you wish to tell

Communication, Language and Literacy

Design-a-cover

Enjoying Stories

• • • • • • • • • •

Resources
- Paper or card
- Pencils
- Crayons
- Felt-tip pens
- Known storybooks

Learning objective
- To provide opportunities for responding to stories

Preparation
- Check the children's knowledge about what the cover of a book is. Have a look at the covers of some of the books that the children know well and discuss what the covers tell them.

What to do
- Read, or tell, a story to the children and talk about the story with them. Who are the important characters? What are the important events? What is the story called' – or can they think of something it might be called?
- Suggest to the children that, if they were going to make a book about the story, they would need to design a cover. Talk about what they might see on the cover of the book – encourage ideas and verbal descriptions.
- Ask the children to design their covers. Take suggestions from them for the title of the book and help them by using strategies for writing, copy-writing, over-copying or scribing the words for them.

Extensions/variations
- Ask each child to share their design with the group, describing it and giving reasons for their choices.
- Make a display of the book covers with a caption giving a short blurb about the book. Read the blurb with the children.

Related activities
- Copy-writing (see page 146)
- Over-copying (see page 141)

Make one like it

Any

All
levels

Learning objectives
● To use a model for creating a story
● To give opportunities for listening to stories with increasing attention and recall

Preparation
● Choose a strongly patterned storybook, such as *Brown Bear, Brown Bear, What Do You See?*

What to do
● Read the book to the children, several times. Encourage them to join in with the choruses and leave gaps for them to fill in.
● Suggest to the children that you all make up your own story, just like the Brown Bear one, using the same pattern, but different ideas.
● Invite suggestions for changing Brown Bear into something else. Point out the alliteration and encourage them to use the same concept – for instance, *Cool Cat*, *Magic Mouse*, *Fat Flea*.
● Carry on making up the story with the children to fit the pattern. The funnier it is, the better. Write their words down as you go along, and read them back with the children.
● When they decide the story is complete, write it on to pages, put it together to make a book and invite the children to illustrate it.

Extensions/variations
● Read the children's new story back with them.
● Get the children to learn and chant the new story as you point to the words.
● Leave the original book and the children's book in an accessible place for sharing and for comparison.

Links to home
● Let the children take turns taking the book home to share with their family.

Resources
■ A strongly patterned storybook, such as *Brown Bear, Brown Bear, What Do You See?* by Bill Martin and Eric Carle (Picture Lions)
■ Flip chart
■ Felt-tip pen
■ Card
■ Paper
■ Treasury tags
■ Hole punch

Communication, Language and Literacy

Making puppets

Enjoying Stories

• • • • • • • • • •

Resources
- A favourite storybook
- Paper bags
- Coloured felt-tip pens
- Bits of fabric and coloured paper
- Glue
- Rubber bands
- Wool or string
- Cardboard box
- Paper plates
- Paper
- Glue

Learning objectives
- To provide opportunities for enjoying stories
- To enhance a story
- To develop awareness of character and event
- To use language to recreate stories

Preparation
- Share a story with the children that they really like.

What to do
- Talk about the characters in the story. Show the children the illustrations and discuss what the characters look like. Who is the children's favourite character? Why? What about the other characters? Who do they like or not like? Can they tell you why? What does each character do? Are they good characters or bad characters? How do they know?
- Suggest that the children make puppets of the characters, so that they can dramatize the story.
- Paper bag puppets are easily made. Invite the children to draw and colour their chosen character on to the bag. Get them to stick on bits and pieces of fabric or coloured paper to make the character even better.
- When the puppets are ready, the paper bag is slipped over the hand and secured around the wrist with a rubber band or piece of wool.
- The children are now all set to re-enact the story with their puppets.

Extensions/variations
- Make a little puppet theatre out of a cardboard box.
- Make the puppets out of paper plate with rolls of paper stuck to the back of them like sticks.
- Ask the children to retell the story to you before they go off to try it out together.

1–4

All levels

Communication, Language and Literacy 119

Chant a story

Learning objective

- To listen with enjoyment and respond to stories

What to do

- Try to find big books with lots of recurring phrases and strong rhythms that the children enjoy. Read the same familiar stories over and over again. Encourage the children to chant along with you as you read, by pointing to different words and pictures. They will begin to associate some of the words with some of the pictures and they will begin to rote-read the passages with you. Eventually they will start to recognize some of the words and phrases and you will be able to remain silent whilst pointing to the words so that the children take over the reading.

Extension/variation

- Encourage the children to share the books in pairs and chant-read them together without any help from you.

Resources

- A collection of stories and books with which the children are familiar
- Large format ('big') books

Understanding stories

Enjoying Stories

• • • • • • • • • •

Resources
- A favourite storybook
- Paper
- Pencils
- Felt-tip pens

Learning objective
- To develop an awareness of how stories work

What to do
- Read, or tell, the story.
- Ask the children to draw you a picture of how the story begins, what happens in the middle and how the story ends.
- Ask the children to put their pictures into the right order and 'read' the story to you in storybook language, from their pictures.

Extensions/variations
- Invite the children to dictate the story to you, for you to scribe on the appropriate pictures. Get the children to put the story into the right order, then stick the three pages together with sticky tape to make a zigzag story book.
- Get the children to read the story back to you and to share it with other children and adults.

Links to home
- Encourage parents to help the children do pictures of home events. Ask the children to bring the pictures to the setting and use them in this activity.

Building stories

Learning objectives
- To show an understanding of the elements of stories, including character, sequencing, openings, etc
- To give opportunities to explore ideas verbally

Preparation
- Make sure that the children have plenty of experience of listening to stories.

What to do
- Sit in a circle with the children. Explain that the object you have in your hand is specially chosen as a–'story-telling ball/car/bear' today. It will help you all to make up a story. You will start, then you will pass the object around the circle. Whoever is holding the object makes up the next bit of the story.
- It is simplest to begin with what you are holding so say, for example, 'Once upon a time, there was a ball. It was…' Describe the ball and give it a situation, for example, 'The ball was bored. It wanted to do something really different. So it took itself off, rolling along the ground'. Then pass the object on to the first child.

- Help the child to make up another bit of the story. Where might the ball have gone to? For example, '*It went all the way to the seaside, over the hills, and rolling down the lanes, until it got to the sea...*' Help the child to stop at a place somewhere in the story where the next child can easily pick it up. For example, '*and along came a gull who said...*'.
- If the children get involved in discussion, allow them to use all their problem-solving skills to continue the story – remind them that *anything* can happen in stories! Make sure that the story has an end.

Extensions/variations
- Get individual children to retell the whole story to a different group of children.
- Do pictures of the story, write key words for the children to recognize.

Resources
- An object to pass round, this could be anything – a ball, car or bear

Picture stories

Enjoying Stories

• • • • • • • • • •

Resources
■ Pictures from magazines, catalogues, posters, etc
■ Paper
■ Writing implements

Learning objectives
● To provide opportunities to predict outcomes and explanations
● To provide opportunities for story-making

Preparation
● Make a collection of pictures that show a scene with something happening.

What to do
● Discuss the pictures. Ask questions.
● Who can we see in the picture? If there are people – are they a family? Who do you think each person is? If there are animals – are they *real* animals or perhaps toy animals? What relationship do they have to each other?
● Where is the event happening? Is it daytime? Night-time? Early morning? Afternoon? Evening? How do we know?
● What things can we see in the picture?
● What might be happening?
● Are they going somewhere? Have they been somewhere?
● What do we think is going to happen next? If this was a story, how would it end?

Extensions/variations
● As the children get used to this kind of activity, get them to try to put their explanations into sentences. Write down the sentences as they are composed, to make a story. At the end, read the story back to the children and ask them if they think they, or you, have missed anything out.

Re-jig a familiar story

4–6

Learning objectives
- To give opportunities to explore ideas and feelings
- To take a familiar story as a base for creating a new one

Preparation
- You need the children to be sitting in a space where they can listen and talk.

What to do
- Tell the children that you were going to do the story of Goldilocks with them, but you're a bit fed up with it, so you wondered whether it would be possible to change it.
- The obvious things to change are:
  - The characters – ie Goldilocks and the bears – Ask the children to decide on their own characters. Maybe they will say something like –'a brave boy and three aliens'.
  - The setting – ie the wood and the little house. Ask the children to make suggestions again. Maybe they will say something like –'a seaside beach and a cave'.

- You could also change the repetitive lines as the children wish, and possibly the outcome, but be guided by the children in this – much will depend upon their level of understanding.

Extensions/variations
- Encourage the children to make a book of their new story.
- Discuss which story the children like best, the original or their new one, and why.

Related activity
- Simply a story (see page 127)

Resources
- A very familiar story, such as *Goldilocks and the Three Bears* – try to link books with topics you are working on at the time (see pages 187–191 for story lines)
- Paper and writing implements to make own book (see Making Books, pages 155–170)

Swapping stories

● ● ● ● ● ● ● ● ●

Resources
■ No special requirements

Learning objectives
● To give opportunities for retelling stories
● To give opportunities for enjoying and sharing stories

Preparation
● Read, or make up, a story that you can easily remember; it needs to be one that is not familiar to the children.

What to do
● Explain to the children what is going to happen. First, you will tell a story to one of the children while the other is doing something else.
● Then the first child will tell the story to the second child, with you listening but not interrupting.
● Then the second child will tell the story back to you, with the first child listening but not interrupting.
● When the story has been told for the last time, you will all discuss the stories and decide whether anything was missed out or added, or if anything was in the wrong order, etc.
● Decide which version of the story is the 'best' version and why. Read or tell the original version to compare it.

Extension/variation
● Get the children to pass on the story to two more children and then discuss the stories again.

Talking about stories

Learning objective
- To develop an understanding of the different elements of stories

What to do
- Read the story to the children, encouraging them to join in if they can and if the story is familiar.
- Afterwards, discuss the story by asking the children questions, such as:
  - ◆ Who, or what, is the story about?
  - ◆ How did the story begin?
  - ◆ How does the story make you feel?
  - ◆ Does it make you feel happy? Or sad?
  - ◆ Why?
  - ◆ Which character do you like best in the story?
  - ◆ Why?
  - ◆ Which character do you like least in the story?
  - ◆ Why?
  - ◆ Which is your favourite part of the story?
  - ◆ Why?
  - ◆ How does the story end?
  - ◆ Is it a good ending?
  - ◆ Why?
  - ◆ What do you think of this story?

Extension/variation
- Ask the children to draw something – an event or a character – from the story and dictate a sentence or two for you to scribe.

Resources
- A selection of known storybooks
- Paper
- Drawing implements

Communication, Language and Literacy

Simply a story

Enjoying Stories

• • • • • • • • • •

Resources
- Computer
- Word processing program
- Paper
- Printer
- Story lines from pages 187–191

Learning objectives
- To give children computer experience
- To link stories with home

What to do
- Choose a simple story line. You could use or expand one of the ones given on pages 187–191, or make up your own.
- Read out the story to the children. Suggest that you give them each a copy of the story to take home to illustrate and share with their family.
- Sit at the computer, with the children around you. Type in the story as you go through it again, with the children helping you to 'remember' it.
- When you have finished typing, read out the story, asking the children to check if you have made any mistakes.
- Print off a copy for each of the children.
- 'Read' through the story again with the children, then send the stories home for the children to illustrate.

Extensions/variations
- Ask the children to bring the stories back so that you can all look at each other's illustrations.
- Make a display of the stories.

Run, run – The Gingerbread Man

Any

Learning objective
- To provide opportunities to listen to stories involving actions

Preparation
- You will need to be familiar with the story of *The Gingerbread Man*.

What to do
- Explain to the children that you are going to tell the story of *The Gingerbread Man* and they are going to be the gingerbread man running away. Can they remember the words he says as he runs?
- Decide on some 'running rules'. For example:
  - Everyone runs in the same direction, without touching anyone else at all.
  - As soon as you say 'And stop' all the gingerbread men stop running and sit down so that you can continue the story. Make sure the children know you will not continue until they are all sitting quietly and ready.

- By the time the children have run away from everyone else and reached the part where they climb on to the fox's back invite them to do their climbing in the space they are already in and lie on the fox's back. When the fox tosses them up into the air, up they jump, and 'make themselves gone' when they land! At this point they need to be totally still and silent so that you can 'see' that there are no gingerbread men left anywhere!

Extensions/variations
- Make a display of the repetitive words eg, 'run, run as fast as you can' and 'read' them with the children.
- Get the children to each do a picture of themselves as *The Gingerbread Man* and display with the words.
- Make and bake gingerbread men. Preheat oven to 180°C/350°F/Gas Mark 4. Line 2 baking trays with baking powder. Cream butter, sugar, golden syrup. Add egg slowly, mix. Add dry ingredients. Mix to dough. Roll out. Cut into shape. Add currants for eyes. Bake for 10 minutes.

Resources
- Story line for *The Gingerbread Man* (see page 190)
- Lots of space
- Paper
- Writing and drawing implements
- Ingredients for gingerbread men:
  125g butter
  60g soft brown sugar
  90g golden syrup
  1 beaten egg
  250g plain flour
  30g self raising flour
  1 tbsp ground ginger
  1 tsp bicarbonate of soda
  1 tbsp currants

© Irene Yates
www.brilliantpublications.co.uk

Making Marks

- The stages in writing development are quite fascinating to watch. These early stages are called 'emergent writing' – the children are beginning to emerge as writers.

- The first stage is 'scribble writing'. It usually has no meaning for anyone except the child who is doing the scribble. But already the writer has understood that written symbols mean messages. She has allocated a message to her scribble. And she has also understood that writing and drawing are two different things. Children at the stage of scribble writing may sometimes scribble letters that you can decipher, and they may also begin to write or copy their name.

- The next stage in emergent writing is 'experimental writing'. The child may be doing something that looks a lot like real writing, although it doesn't make any sense. It shows that the writer understands that speech can be written down, and that she knows that the message remains the same once it is written in symbols. Children at this stage are also beginning to understand that, in English, the symbols go from left to right and down the page. They often experiment with writing letters and words. They can usually 'read' their message back to you and, at some point during this stage, you may be able to work out what some of the words are – for instance 'su' for 'saw'.

- While the children are developing their skills as emergent writers, you can give them lots of help by giving them opportunities for copying and tracing. You can 'scribe' their messages for them – ask what they want to write and show them how you write it, then help them to read it back. Model the writing process for them, saying, for example, 'Now I'm going to write your name. We start with a B – down, up, round, into the middle, and round again,' and so on. You are modelling the writing process when you say, for example, 'What word comes next? What sound does it start with? How do we write that sound?' because you are showing the children the thought processes that are involved in writing.

- After the emergent writing stage the writers continue to develop, beginning to understand the way letters need to be formed and that 'spelling' is important. They then move on to using punctuation and planning their writing. Finally they become proficient writers, but, of course, they may take many years to reach this point.

- The point of 'making marks' at the Foundation Stage is to help the children to understand that they *can become* proficient writers, and to give them lots of practice in exercizing their skills, and lots of positive reinforcement and feedback to motivate them to want to become writers.

Keeping a writing record

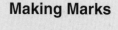

(1–2)

(All levels)

Learning objective
- To encourage writing development

Preparation
- Make a notebook for each child, showing their name clearly. Keep them where they are accessible to the children so that they can do some 'writing' at any time of the session. Encourage them to be independent in this aspect.

What to do
- Explain to the children that the notebooks are for them to record their ideas, messages and stories in. Show them which is the right-hand page of each double-page spread. The right-hand side is *their* side, the left-hand side is *your* side.
- Encourage them to write messages, stories, etc, whenever they want to, on the right-hand page, and perhaps draw a picture underneath the message, to illustrate it.
- On the left-hand page, write the date the message was written, decode the message (with the child's help) and record any information you feel is important, such as comments on any skill development or ideas for future teaching.
- At the end of the term or year you will have a see-at-a-glance record of the child's writing development.

Extensions/variations
- The children do not need to 'read' every scribble story to you for you to write the interpretation – you can get them to 'read' some of their messages into a tape recorder instead.
- Give suggestions for stories or messages they might write in their books from work you are doing in other areas of learning.

Resources
- A small notebook for each child
- Pencils
- Felt-tip pens
- Crayons
- Writing tools always available
- Tape recorder
- Blank cassette tape

Communication, Language and Literacy

Write it right!

Making Marks

• • • • • • • • • •

Resources
- Paper
- Thick pencils
- Pencil grips
- Rule
- Forming letters template (see page 179)

Learning objective
● To give opportunities to develop skills of writing

Preparation
● Draw sets of three lines on paper. Two lines approximately 2cm apart, with another line 7mm above the top line.
● Practise writing the letters yourself so that you know the exact movements. Use the template on page 179.

What to do
● It is important that the children learn the correct formation of the letters from the beginning. Once they have learnt to do them wrong, for example starting at the wrong place or going in the wrong direction, it will be next to impossible for them to 'unlearn'.
● They need to be taught that each whole letter is written in one go. The only letters for which they should take the pencil from the page before completing them are the k, the x, to dot the i and j and to cross the t and f.
● Make up little mantras to say with them as they are forming the letters. For example, for a, you might say, 'Start over here, backwards and round, down, round at the bottom, up, up, up (don't take your pencil off) and down again, add a little tail.' This will really help them to get fixed in their head how each letter should be formed.

● Don't tackle too many letters at once. Start with the letters of their names and only add more letters as you see how they are progressing.

Extensions/variations
● Add capital letters only when the children need them, for example for their initials.
● Really able children will be interested in the alphabet and its order, but don't worry the ones who aren't.

Links to home
● If you can make an opportunity to show parents how letters should be formed, you will be giving the children lots of additional help. Perhaps you could run a 'Writing half-hour' to show them how important this is.

Writing notes

Learning objective
4–6
- To attempt writing for different purposes – using different forms

Preparation
All levels
- Make some notes of your own on self-stick notes. It's useful to use self-stick notes when you are talking or observing the children and you want to remind yourself of something you need to record about them, instead of breaking off to record. Make notes on the self-stick notes, stick them in a space (wall or window) and collect them up at the end of the day. If the children see you doing this often they will become aware of the usefulness of notes.

What to do
- Explain to the children why you make your notes, so that you won't forget something important. Discuss how writing notes is not the same as writing stories, even though it is still writing. Can the children explain why? Tell the children that you are going to give them all some self-stick notes so that, during the session, they can make their own notes to remind them of things they want to tell you. Show them where to stick their notes. Write each child's name on the corner so that you know which belongs to whom. Give the children freedom to make the notes when they wish.

- At the end of the session, gather the notes and the children together. Delegate a child to collect all the notes and hand them out to the appropriate child (you might have to read some of the names).
- Get each child to 'read' their notes to the group. Discuss the usefulness of the activity with them.

Extensions/variations
- Instead of leaving the children to 'write' their own notes, help them to write in whichever way is appropriate for their stage of development, ie scribbling, tracing, copying, etc.
- Help them to read the notes back.
- Use concepts from other areas as the focus points of specific notes. For example, say, 'Liam, could you write a note to remind us to check whether leaves turn gold in the autumn, please,' or whatever.

Resources
- Self-stick notes
- Pencils

Communication, Language and Literacy

Chalk-a-line

Making Marks

• • • • • • • • • •

Resources

- Large floor or outside paved area
- Chalk
- Cloth and spray bottle of water for cleaning up

Learning objectives

- To enjoy manipulating writing and drawing tools
- To develop fine motor control

Preparation

- Make sure the children know which area they are allowed to use the chalk in.

What to do

- Show the children how to draw shapes, lines and dots with the chalk. Just give them the opportunity to have fun drawing shapes or squiggly lines, walking along them, running from one dot or mark to another, and creating new images.
- The idea is to encourage them to enjoy making their own marks, and to develop a good flow, as well as freedom of expression.
- Use the spray bottle and cloth to clean up after you.

Extensions/variations

- As hand/eye coordination develops, suggest shapes for the children to draw and walk round, on or along.
- Draw a hopscotch area with numbers and show the children how to play.

3–5

Communication, Language and Literacy

Controlled scribble

Making Marks

● ● ● ● ● ● ● ● ●

Learning objectives

- To develop hand/eye coordination
- To develop fine motor control
- To give opportunities for developing writing skills

Preparation

- Have the writing tools all ready, with the paper on a flat or slanted surface.

What to do

- Observe how the children move from uncontrolled scribbling to more controlled efforts.
- Encourage left to right movements.
- Encourage circle shapes, straight lines and squiggly lines.
- Use the language of writing symbols and shapes, such as 'round', 'upwards', 'downwards', 'straight', 'squiggly', 'dot', 'top', 'bottom', etc.
- Ask: 'What are you going to draw/write? Where will you start? Which way will your pen/crayon go?'
- Give the children plenty of time to explore what they can do.
- When the children have finished, discuss their writing/drawing with them. Let them see you writing on their product, 'This is (name)'s picture of…' or '(name)'s story says…'. Read your words back to them, pointing to them as you read.

Extensions/variations

- Add to the collection of each child's pieces.
- Link to other areas by suggesting content that ties in with topics you are exploring currently with the children.

Resources

- Large pieces of paper
- Large writing tools: felt-tip pens, crayons, paintbrushes, etc

Make a necklace

Making Marks

Resources
- Pieces of string or wool
- Breakfast cereal with holes in
- Flip chart
- Felt-tip pen

Learning objectives
- To develop hand/eye coordination
- To write simple instructions

What to do
- Show the children how to make a necklace by threading breakfast cereal on to the wool or string. Tie the ends so that the necklace will go over the children's heads.
- Tell the children that you would like to write some instructions for other children on how to make the necklaces.
- Ask the children to help you to compose a title for the instructions. The instructions need to be in two parts, *What you need* and *What you do.* Write down the first heading, reading the words back with the children. Take suggestions from them for the list and scribe them, reading the words back with the children. Write the second heading and repeat the process.

Extensions/variations
- Invite the children to explain to other children or adults how they made their necklaces.
- Ask the children to 'read' their instructions to other children or adults.
- Use this technique to get the children to help you write instructions for other things, for example, how to feed the guinea pig, etc.

3

Sand-writing

Learning objective
- To give opportunities for the children to practise writing letter shapes

What to do
- Show the children how they might draw pictures or write letters in the sand with a finger. Encourage them to experiment with writing different letter sounds that they know. Get them to do the letters with a finger in the air first so that they are sure where the letters start and end.
- Invite them to explore the differences between writing in the wet sand and in the dry sand: 'What happens to the sand? How different does it feel to your finger? Do the letters stay the same? Could we write our names in the sand? Would we be able to write a whole message in the sand? Would it be the same as writing a message on paper? Why? What would happen to it?'

- Help them to write their own names and their friends' names so that they are covering a wide range of letters.

Extension/variation
- Experiment with making letters in different ways. Help the children to shape letters out of dough or Plasticine, or cut out coloured paper.

Resources
- Wet and/or dry sand trays
- Dough or Plasticine
- Coloured paper
- Scissors

Scribble scribble

Making Marks

• • • • • • • • • •

Resources
- Large pieces of paper
- Big writing tools like fat crayons and fat felt-tip pens that do not need a lot of pressure in order to make marks
- Chubby pencils
- Rubber pencil grips for the children that need them

Learning objectives
- To develop hand/eye coordination
- To develop fine motor control
- To encourage use of writing materials

Preparation
- Have all the materials ready, with the paper on a flat or slanted surface. Sometimes it helps children if the paper is at an angle so that they do not have to use too much pressure with the tools.
- Help the children to hold the writing tools correctly.
- Accept right- or left-handed use of tools.

What to do
- Encourage the children to experiment with random and uncontrolled scribbling, making indiscriminate marks on the surface of the paper. Encourage movements in all directions – up/down, down/up, right/left, left/right, diagonally – whatever the child feels happy to do. Use the vocabulary of different directions so that the children absorb the language.
- Give plenty of time for them to explore.
- Ask: 'Is it a picture? What is it of? Is it writing? What does it say?' and listen attentively for each child's comments on their own work.
- Show the children how you write their names (pointing out letters and sounds where appropriate) and the date on their 'writing'.

Extensions/variations
- Start a collection of dated 'writing' for each child and add to it every two weeks or so. This will enable you to keep a Record of Achievement and to follow the child's progress.
- Suggest topics for the child's content that fit in with other areas you are exploring. For example, if you have been looking at mini beasts you could say, 'Why don't you write about the snails we saw?'

4–6

Sky-writing

Making Marks

● ● ● ● ● ● ● ● ●

Learning objectives

- To practise letter shapes
- To reinforce the correct way to form letters

Preparation

- Do this activity at any time when the children have begun to build up their knowledge of letter shapes.

What to do

- Have the children sitting or standing in a group with you standing in front of them. Tell them you are going to show them how to do *sky-writing*, which is writing letters in the air with a finger.
- Choose a child whose name you can write in the air.
- You need to stand with your back to the children so that you are all facing the same way. Ask the children what sound the child's name begins with. Write it in the air, describing it as you go, for example, 'Shazia's name begins with S, the sound "s". We start at the top, go backwards and round, then forwards and round and backwards again.'
- Repeat the first letter, then go on to the next one, and so on.

Extensions/variations

- When the children can do quite a few letters, ask them to do them as big as they can, using their whole arm and shoulder instead of just one finger.
- Then do them as tiny as they can, as though on their thumbnail. All the time, verbalize the correct way to form the letter shape.
- Encourage the children to say the direction words to themselves quietly when they are using implements.

Related activity

- Write it right! (see page 131)

Resources

- No special requirements

Communication, Language and Literacy

Watch out!

Making Marks

• • • • • • • • • •

Resources
■ Card
■ Felt-tip pen

Learning objective
● To write labels and captions and begin to form simple sentences

What to do
● When you are talking to the whole group tell them that you are thinking about ideas for putting signs around your setting. For example, you may need a sign that says, 'Only two children in the water, please.' Ask the children to look around, while they are playing indoors and outside, to see if there is anywhere that needs a sign of any kind.
● Leave the card and the pen in a place that's accessible for the children and encourage them to have a go at making a sign when they find somewhere that needs one. When they have made a sign, they should read it to you.
● Encourage imaginative thinking and help the children to display their signs in appropriate places.

Extensions/variations
● Encourage the children to construct messages that are important to them – *'Don't scare the birds away, Don't climb the tree, No fighting for bikes'*, and so on.
● Help the children to formulate a range of rules for keeping safe and happy.

Related activity
● Marks for meaning (see page 147)

ONLY TWO CHILDREN IN THE WATER PLEASE

Have a go

Learning objective
(1–6)
- To use phonic knowledge to write simple regular words

Preparation
- Set up the flip chart or easel so that all the children can see it easily. Have an idea in your head for a story, shared event or personal experience you and the children can write about together. For example, you may have been on a trip to the shops or the park, which would be a good stimulus.

What to do
- Tell the children that you are all going to write your 'story' together, that you will do most of the writing but that you know they will be able to do some of it, too. Discuss what you are going to write about.

- Invite the children to think up a title, or heading, for the writing. When you have come to a consensus, ask if any of the children can write any of those words – they may be able to have a stab at 'the', 'at', 'to', etc. Write some of the words yourself and get the children out to write the words they want to attempt. Some children may only want to have a go at certain letters, rather than words, that's fine. Give lots of praise and encouragement for their efforts.

- Make sure you point out the spaces that have to be left between words. Carry on in this way until the 'story' has been written.
- Read it back, all together.

Extension/variation
- Work with individual children in the same way, encouraging them to take over the writing whenever they feel able, so that you are writing together in an 'apprenticeship' manner (see page 129).

Resources
- Large sheet of paper
- Black felt-tip pen
- Easel or flip chart

Communication, Language and Literacy

© Irene Yates
www.brilliantpublications.co.uk

Over-copying

Making Marks

• • • • • • • • •

Resources
- ■ Paper
- ■ Pencils
- ■ Felt-tip pens
- ■ Highlighter pens

Learning objective
- To give opportunities to develop skills of over-copying, or tracing over, writing

Preparation
- Talk about something that the children have been doing, or something that has been happening in the group, or a story that you have shared with them, so that the children have an idea of something that they could compose a 'story' about.

What to do
- Recap the event with the children and ask them to each think about how they could illustrate it. Give the children paper and tools to do their pictures. Ask them to think about the text that might go with their picture. Help them to put their ideas into simple sentences – if they only want one sentence, that's fine.
- Work with each child individually. Scribe, in light pencil and big letters, the sentence(s) or caption(s) that they have composed, demonstrating how you do the writing as you go along – 'We start here and write…', showing direction and reading the words back with them. The main thing is for the children to know exactly what they are over-copying as they do it, and to be able to attempt to read the text back.

- Give each child time to over-copy, or trace, their composed text, and help them to read it back again, then have a sharing time when each child shares their story with the rest of the small group.

Extensions/variations
- Instead of doing 'light' pencil work, write a dotted version for the children to go over. Alternatively use a highlighter pen.
- Write out the children's favourite nursery rhymes for them to trace and illustrate. They can take them home, make a display of them, or turn them into a nursery rhyme book.

Communication, Language and Literacy

Send an e-mail

Learning objective
- To give opportunities to send and receive messages by e-mail

Preparation
- Make sure you have introduced the children to the computer (see page 25).

What to do
- When the children have written letters to each other and to other people, introduce them to the idea of sending an e-mail. Explain that an e-mail is very much like a letter; it is a message you send to somebody else but instead of putting it into an envelope and posting it in the post box for the post delivery person to deliver, you send it yourself, via a mail server, from one computer to another.
- Decide on the person who is to receive the e-mail. Set the e-mail up yourself, explaining what you are doing. Make sure you are using a large-sized font so that the children can 'read' it. Discuss what your message should be. Let the children have a turn in keying in some of the message with your help. When you have read the message back together and the children are satisfied, let one of them click on 'send'.
- With the children, check that the recipient received the e-mail and await a reply.

Extension/variation
- Make sending and receiving e-mails a regular activity. You could join forces with another group to do this.

Links to home
- Find out if there are any parents willing to swap e-mails with the group occasionally.

Resources
- Computer
- Internet link
- e-mail address(es) of people prepared to correspond with children by e-mail

Communication, Language and Literacy

Making Marks

● ● ● ● ● ● ● ● ● ●

Resources
- Strong card
- Scissors
- Hole punch
- Coloured wool

Learning objectives
- To develop hand/eye coordination
- To develop fine motor control

Preparation
- Cut the card into shapes appropriate to other key areas or topics you are working on. For instance, if you are doing a shapes topic, cut out geometrical shapes; if you are looking at animals, cut out simple animal shapes.
- Use the hole punch to punch a pattern of holes around the edges.

What to do
- Give each child a card shape and let them choose some coloured wool. Show them how to thread the wool in and out through the punched holes. Use appropriate vocabulary all the time – *in and out, through, back, front, over* – to reinforce the children's understanding of the words.
- This activity will help children to develop the pincer movement they need to hold a pencil properly.

Extensions/variations
- Help the children to cut out their own shapes of card and make the holes where they want them.
- Thread several different colours of wool through the holes to make more complex patterns.

Signing in

Making Marks

● ● ● ● ● ● ● ● ● ●

Learning objective
● To write their own names

Preparation
● Draw shapes on the sheet of card which are big enough for each child to write their name in.

What to do
● Tell the children that you sometimes do not know who's arrived and who hasn't because you are busy saying hello to other people or doing something else, but it would be very handy if the children could 'sign in' when they arrive at the group.
● Show them where you are going to put the card – it needs to be on a flat or slanted surface but not a wall. Discuss with them the possibility of the pen going missing and show them how you are going to tie it to the string and sticky-tape the string to the card, to keep the pen in one place.

● Invite the children to practise writing their name in a space – if they cannot do their name encourage them to make a mark that represents their name.
● It will only take a few minutes to make a new piece of card for each day. Draw different shapes to contain the names – clouds, circles, triangles, sheep, cats, etc, and when the children go home ask them if they can guess what the shapes might be for the next day.

Extension/variation
● Have a card with each child's name written on it, and a box. Instead of writing their names, the children find their own name and place it in the box.

Related activity
● This is me (see page 150)

Resources
■ Large sheet of card
■ Black felt-tip pen
■ String
■ Sticky tape

© Irene Yates
www.brilliantpublications.co.uk

Special writing

Making Marks

• • • • • • • • • •

Resources
- Large sheet of paper
- Coloured felt-tip pens
- Small piece of card
- Black felt-tip pen

Learning objective
- To provide opportunities for the children to practise writing

Preparation
- Put the sheet of paper on a writing surface, with lots of coloured felt pens.

What to do
- Tell the children that you would like them to make a big writing display to put on the wall for the parents to see. They may say that they 'cannot write' but emphasize that you want them to do their own special kind of writing and that they may do it how they wish.
- Leave the children to choose their colours and decide how they want to do the writing and let them get on with it. The writing may turn out to be squiggles or letters or scribbles, it is all acceptable.
- Write a caption on the card, showing the names of the children and reporting that they 'did all of this writing'. Display it in a prominent place. Look at it with the rest of the children and read the caption to them.

Extensions/variations
- Give the children opportunities to experiment with writing in outside situations – either on paper and card or on paving slabs and other surfaces, so that they understand that print can happen in all places, not just inside on a table or desk!
- When you have studied a specific topic, ask children to write 'about it' in the same way; change your caption to read 'x and x did all this writing about … (whatever the topic is)'.

© Irene Yates
www.brilliantpublications.co.uk

Copy-writing

① Learning objective

- To give opportunities to develop skills of copy-writing

Preparation

- Set up activities that will give the children opportunities for writing – for example, playing post offices, schools, etc.

What to do

- Sit with the child, discussing what needs to be written – it may be a sentence, a caption, a list. – Make it relevant to the activity the child is taking part in.
- Draw a line across the sheet of paper. Ask the child to dictate to you what she wants to write. Write the child's message carefully and slowly across the top half of the paper, making sure you leave noticeable gaps between words. The copying space is below; the child needs to be able to copy each letter/word underneath. If you write more than one line, make sure there is space to copy the first line before you start the next line. Read the message back with the child, pointing to the words as you go along.
- Show the child where to copy, and let her get on with it. Try not to intervene – it is important at this stage that she carries out the task with confidence and feels that she is able to do it.
- Read the child's message back with her.

Extensions/variations

- Use the copying technique for short messages. Don't expect the child to try to copy long pieces of text.
- Use the copying technique for children to learn to write their own names; write their name for them and give them space to copy underneath.
- When they are really good at copying, give longer texts of two or three sentences.

Resources

- Paper
- Writing implements

Communication, Language and Literacy

© Irene Yates
www.brilliantpublications.co.uk

Marks for meaning

Making Marks

Resources
- Toy and tool boxes, shelves, drawers, etc, where you store the equipment used with the group
- Card
- Writing implements

Learning objective
- To develop the children's awareness that they can ascribe meanings to marks

Preparation
- Mix up some of the tools or equipment, so that it needs to be sorted into its appropriate sets.

What to do
- Ask the children to help you sort out the tools or equipment. Ask them how you and they could be sure that when anyone uses them they would all go into the right place. Guide them towards the suggestion that if boxes, drawers, etc were labelled then everyone would know where everything should go.
- Suggest that you write new labels together for the sets you have made.
- Ask the children to suggest what should go on the labels. Rather than just 'pencils' (for example), get them to suggest a sentence such as 'Put the pencils in here.'
- Write each label carefully, with the children observing. As you write, ask the children which sound the words begin and end with. If some are at the stage where they can write any of the letters ask them to show you how they go by writing them with their fingers in the air (see Sky-writing, page 138).
- At the end of the session, read back all the labels, carefully, with the children.

Extensions/variations
- Write one-word labels, eg 'pencils', 'crayons', 'balls', etc. Encourage children to match the words with the words on the labels.
- Encourage the children to 'read' the labels when putting things away. They will probably recognize the right container from other cues, but reinforcing the written words each time helps to create awareness.

Modelling writing

Learning objective

- To use opportunities to model writing in order to increase the children's awareness

Preparation

- Set up activities that give you the opportunity to model, or demonstrate, writing, such as making books, writing stories, writing lists, writing notes, etc.

What to do

- Important points for writing for children to learn at this stage are:
  - ◆ that we write in a left to right direction
  - ◆ that sounds and shapes (letters) are connected
  - ◆ that we always write the shapes (letters) in the same way
  - ◆ that there are gaps between words
  - ◆ that the words say the same thing no matter how many times we read them.
- If you 'model' the writing as you are doing it, the children pick up these concepts without even knowing it.

- For example, if you were writing a child's name, you would say, 'What sound does it begin with? Where shall we start? Which way shall we go? How do we do this letter? We do a line down, a line across for the T. What's the next sound? It's an "o". We start here and go backwards and round. What's the last sound? It's a "mmm"' (try not to say 'muh'.), *'To do a "m" we start here, go down, go up and over, down again, up and over and down.'*
- It isn't necessary to model every single bit of every single piece of writing, but lots of consistent modelling soon means the children absorb the early concepts and will often be willing to have a go themselves.

Extension/variation

- Use modelling to write group pieces, and always get the children to 'read back' with you what has been composed and scribed.

Multicultural link

- Some languages are not written from left to right (eg Arabic, Hebrew, Chinese). Collect examples to show the children if you can.

Resources

- Paper
- Writing implements

Make a card

Making Marks

• • • • • • • • • •

Resources
- Card
- Pens
- Pencils
- Crayons
- Paper
- Scissors
- Glue
- Stickers
- Odds and ends of craft materials

Learning objectives
- To give the children opportunities for creating and writing simple messages
- To help children understand the importance of messages

What to do
- All sorts of celebrations will arise over the academic year – birthdays, name days, Mother's Day, Father's Day, religious festivals, etc. There is nothing more satisfying to children than to make a special greetings card for the occasion. They often learn to write 'love from' and their name without even thinking about it!
- Each child needs a decent piece of card folded in half. It is helpful to buy good materials for the activity because the more attractive the card is, the more effort the children will put into their greetings. Help the children to decide on wording appropriate to the occasion.
- The children will be at different stages of ability – be prepared to write the words for them, to write them so that they can copy them, to write them so that they can over-copy them. Give them lots of encouragement to have a go at writing their words by themselves. If necessary, write an interpretation somewhere on the card.

- Encourage the children to think of good ways of illustrating their cards. This can be by drawing or cutting and sticking – glitter-sticking always goes down very well. While the children are doing this they are developing their skills of hand/eye coordination.
- All the time the children are engaged in this activity you should be talking them through it so that they are learning lots of language and vocabulary.

Extension/variation
- Get the children to show their cards individually to the group, and describe them. Ask the group for comments – what do they like about each card?

Links to home
- Encourage the children to make cards at home to send to their friends at the group.

Multicultural link
- Be aware of different ethnic festivals that you can celebrate together.

Related activity
- Send a letter (see page 68)

Any

This is me

Making Marks
• • • • • • • • • • •

Learning objective
- To develop ability to write own name

Preparation
- Have the paper and writing tools ready for the children to work with. At the top of each child's sheet, write 'This is me'. At the bottom of the sheet, write 'My name is' and a line for the child to write their name on.

What to do
- Explain to the children what the words at the top and bottom of the page say. Give them each a sticky label and tell them that this is for them to write their name on; when they are satisfied with their writing then they can stick the label in the appropriate space.
- Ask the children to draw a picture of themselves on the paper and colour it in. Go round the group, helping each child to write her name. Involve the children sitting close to her, by asking 'What sound does Emma's name begin with? Does anyone know how to write the letter? Where shall we start it?', etc.

- Make sure that the children are holding their pencils correctly; try to provide chubby pencils, triangular pencils or rubber pencil holders for any child who has problems with this. Decide which kind of writing would be best for each child – over-copying, copying, scribing, or you making the sounds and showing them.
- Encourage the children to learn the shapes of the letters of their name, as well as the sounds. Get them to compare any letters that are the same as letters in someone else's name.
- Make a display of the self-portraits.

Extensions/variations
- Ask the children to draw and colour pictures for their parents and help them to write their own names on them.
- Get the children used to writing their own name on each piece of work they do in any of the areas.
- Help the children to develop the pincer movement they need to hold a pencil properly by doing threading activities.

Resources
- Paper
- Pencils
- Crayons
- Felt-tip pens
- Sticky labels

Write me a letter

Making Marks

• • • • • • • • • •

Resources
- Paper
- Black felt-tip pen

Learning objective
- To give opportunities to practise writing for different purposes

Preparation
- If possible, set up a play situation where a natural outcome would be for a letter to be written, for example someone in hospital, someone on a visit, someone on holiday.

What to do
- Suggest to the child that she writes a letter appropriate to the situation. For example, if someone is in hospital she might write to ask how they are and send her best wishes and promise to go and see them. Suggest that she makes up the letter, tells you what it needs to say and that you write down the words for her.
- Prompt the child gently and give her plenty of time to verbalize her thoughts and get them into the right order – she will be practising the skills of composition, staying on task and sequencing, as well as observing you using appropriate punctuation and grammar as her message is recorded.

- Encourage the child to write her own name and any other words she can write at the end of the letter.
- Read it back carefully, with the child, pointing to the words as you go and encourage the child to read it back again to you.

Extension/variation
- Use this dictation technique to write:
  - stories
  - shopping lists
  - stories about events in the children's lives.

Related activity
- Send an e-mail (see page 142)

Taking messages

Learning objective
1–2
- To give opportunities to link the idea of spoken words with written words

Preparation
- Invite the children into a role play situation with you where one of you needs to give a message and the other one needs to write it down.

What to do
- Talk about message-taking situations. The children may have lots that they can think of – or may not have seen and heard anyone taking messages. The more situations you can imagine with the children, the better, because you will be feeding in lots of new vocabulary and language.
- For example, you might be telephoning the doctor or the dentist to make an appointment, or telephoning the florist to arrange for some flowers to be delivered, or telephoning home to remind someone to video your favourite programme – make the story as interesting as you can.
- Decide which of you is going to take the message and which is going to give it. Have a clear message worked out between you to begin with.

- Encourage the children to 'write' the message in any way they can. Read the message back together.

Extensions/variations
- Have a session where the children talk together about what they have been doing in their message-taking games and show each other their messages.
- Encourage the children to learn how to give their name and address clearly on the phone, and how to ring emergency services.

Related activity
- Make a call (see page 35)

Resources
- Old phones, mobiles, pretend phones, etc
- Note pads
- Self-stick notes
- Pencils

Communication, Language and Literacy

Message in a bottle

Making Marks

• • • • • • • • • •

Resources
- Paper
- Pencils
- Felt-tip pen
- Plastic bottle

Learning objectives
- To attempt writing for different purposes
- To develop an awareness of print

Preparation
- Look for opportunities for the children to role play being pirates.

What to do
- Explain to the children how pirates trapped on an island might be desperate to send somebody a message so that they could rescue them. How could the pirates send the message? No computers or e-mail, no post boxes, no phones or mobiles, nobody calling to take a message.
- Suggest that the pirates could put a message in a bottle and throw it into the sea. The sea would wash the bottle away and send it to another land where someone would find it and be able to rescue them.
- What might the message say?
- Help the children to each 'write' a message. Let them do this in any way they want, don't try to get them to do letters/sounds or words unless they are ready to. They may merely want to do a scrawl across the page – that's fine. Give them plenty of positive feedback for their attempt at writing. Get them to read back to you what they have made their message say. Put the messages in the bottle, seal it and let them 'cast it into the sea' (or at least roll it across the floor!) from the island.

Extensions/variations
- Line up an adult with a different group of children to receive the messages and organize a rescue party.
- In circle time, have the children, in role, recount their experiences and show their messages.

Related activities
- Be a pirate (see page 73)
- Treasure map (see page 154)

4–6

All levels

Treasure map

2–3

All levels

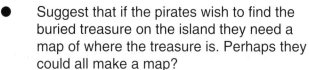

Learning objectives
● To attempt writing for different purposes
● To develop an awareness of what writing means

Preparation
● Have pirate role play activities available.

What to do
● Show the children your map and ask if they know what it is. Have they ever seen maps? When do adults use maps? What are they for?
● Suggest that if the pirates wish to find the buried treasure on the island they need a map of where the treasure is. Perhaps they could all make a map?
● Talk them through making their maps – they need to do the shoreline of the island, perhaps draw a tree, put in anything else they think is important to show the pirates where to go, put a cross where the treasure is and 'write' on their map, 'The treasure is here'.

● Be happy to accept whatever marks they want to make. If they want you to help by writing certain letters or words, you can scribe for them. Some children may want you to do words or symbols for them to trace over.

Extensions/variations
● Colour the maps.
● Make maps of your own setting.

Related activities
● Be a pirate (see page 73)
● Message in a bottle (see page 153)

Resources
■ Pirate activities
■ Large sheets of paper
■ Pens or crayons
■ A simple map to show children how a map works

Making Books

- The aim of making books with children is to give them lots of opportunities for reading and writing material that they own themselves. They will be so proud of the books they have made that they will want to show them to everyone they know, share them and read them to themselves over and over again.

- The one thing children need in order to develop their literacy skills is practice. The one thing that children (or anyone!) need in order to write is a reason to do so. Making books covers each of these criteria.

- Making books about events that are important to the children give them a sense for recording their experiences. Always have lots of different kinds of paper available, lots of different writing tools. Give the children every opportunity to cut and stick pictures that are appropriate to their chosen text, and take photographs to illustrate their recordings of things they have done in the group.

- Making books together is a good creative activity that can be non-threatening and undemanding, it can help you and them to connect with each other and communicate. As well as deciding upon the words and pictures they want in their books, the children will extend their speaking skills by exploring materials and selecting supplies, planning and negotiating how they want the book to be.

- Making books is such a wonderful language activity, the children all enjoy it and more often than not want to go on to make books of their own, independently. Encourage them to develop their skills whenever time permits, and then sit down to enjoy the results together.

Easy peasy book

Learning objectives

- To give opportunities to incorporate literacy into all areas of learning
- To make a simple book

Preparation

- The preparation is whatever activity you have been working on with the children. Get them to draw and 'write' their experiences.

What to do

- Help with tracing, copying and emergent writing where necessary. Scribe words that children ask you to write for them, or specifically ask them to compose and dictate words to you. Make sure their individual name is on each piece of work.
- Take two pieces of card for the book's 'covers' and punch a hole through the top left-hand corner. Assemble the pages. Punch a hole straight through the top left-hand corner.
- Put the pages inside the covers, give the front cover a title and the group's name as author and illustrator. Hang the book where the children can reach it easily, to read and share. The book will lie flat and will be easy to open.

Extensions/variations

- Give the children plenty of opportunity to share the book with each other.
- You can make books specific to any of the key areas by choosing to use particular activities as the content.

Links to home

- Encourage them to take it home to share with their parents.

Resources

- Paper
- Card
- Hole punch
- Scissors
- String

Communication, Language and Literacy

Make a sound book

Making Books

• • • • • • • • •

Resources

- A3 paper or card
- Old catalogues/ magazines
- Glue
- Scissors
- Felt-tip pens
- Ring clips
- Hole punch

Learning objectives

- To identify sounds and letters
- To incorporate literacy into all areas of learning
- To show how pictures and texts link

Preparation

- Make this book after you have done some work on 'beginning' sounds.

What to do

- Suggest to the children that they make a book of things beginning with the same sound. Discuss which sound they would like to work on and come to an agreement.
- Look for things in the catalogues/magazines which begin with the chosen sound. Cut out and stick a few items to each page. As the children are working on the task, keep reinforcing the sound and its shape.
- Help the children to finger-trace the letter in the air.
- On the cover, write the title: *Our book of 's' things* (or whichever sound they are doing), and an authorship.
- Number the pages with the children, reminding them that you do not have a number on the cover or inside cover and that page 1 is the first right-hand page.

- Punch holes and secure.
- Read the book with the children, naming and talking about the things on their pages.

Extension/variation

- Stick to single consonants and vowels where you can, but with more able children you could work on double consonants (such as 'll') and clusters (such as 'str', cl).

Photo albums

Learning objectives

- To record a significant event in the group's life
- To incorporate literacy into all areas of learning
- To show how pictures and texts link

Preparation

- Choose an event of some importance to the group. For example, a trip, a walk, a visit, a party, etc. Take lots of photographs of the children and the things that interest them.

What to do

- To assemble the book you will need to have pictures on the left-hand page and text on the right-hand page.
- With small groups of children at a time, stick one photograph to each left-hand page. For the right-hand page, ask the children what they would like to say about the photo and demonstrate writing simple text.
- Decide on a title. Make the front and back covers out of card, write the title and give an authorship.
- With the children's help, assemble the pages in order, taking care of the sequence. Number the pages.
- Punch holes and secure with ring clips.

Extensions/variations

- Share the book often with the children, getting them to discuss the pictures and 'read' the text with you.
- Make the book available for 'reading' times and encourage the children to read it together.

Links to home

- Give the children opportunities to take the book home.

Resources

- Camera
- An occasion to photograph
- Card or sugar paper
- Felt-tip pens
- Glue
- Ring clips

Re-tell a story

Making Books

• • • • • • • • • •

Resources
- A3 sheets of coloured paper
- Lots of A6 paper (A4 cut into quarters)
- Felt-tip pens
- Crayons
- Glue
- Hole punch
- Ring clips or treasury tags

Learning objectives
- To incorporate literacy into all areas of learning
- To show how pictures and texts link
- To develop sequencing skills

Preparation
- Choose a story the children know and love.

What to do
- Talk about the chosen story. Encourage the children to get all the events into the right order. Suggest that together you make a book, telling the story.
- Give each child a piece of A6 to draw a picture illustrating what she chooses as the first event.
- Select some of the pictures to stick to the first left-hand page. Ask the children to help you decide on text for the right-hand page. Keep it very simple, one or two sentences only, and write it in large text, saying the words as you write.
- Point out where you start and which direction you write in. Point out the full stop at the end of the sentence(s).
- Repeat these steps until you get to the end of the story.

- When the pages are finished, number them with the children's help. Decide on a title and authorship for the cover page.
- Check that the events and words are in the right order, punch holes down the left-hand side and secure the pages with ring clips or treasury tags. (You can use string or wool but you will find the pages do not lie flat.)

Extensions/variations
- Read the book with individuals, pairs or small groups.
- Make the book available for the children to share when they wish.
- Make a book yourself of a story the children love, and introduce it to them.

Links to home
- Encourage the children take the book home to share with their parents.

the monster roared

A simple flap book

Learning objectives
- To incorporate literacy into all areas of learning
- To show how pictures and texts link

Preparation

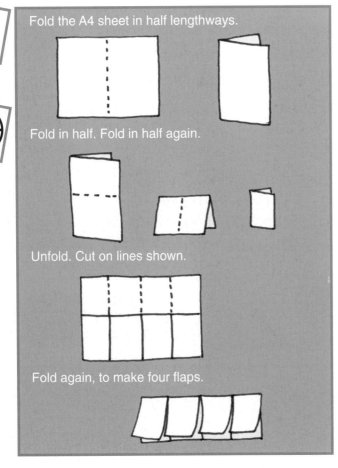

Fold the A4 sheet in half lengthways.

Fold in half. Fold in half again.

Unfold. Cut on lines shown.

Fold again, to make four flaps.

What to do
- Show the child how the flaps work and explain that together you will make it into a book. Discuss a topic for the four pages.
- For example on page 1 you might want: *What colour is the crocodile?* Then, under the flap draw a crocodile, colour it red and write: *The crocodile is red.*
- Continue your chosen theme for the four pages and flaps. Join the folded edges together with sticky tape.
- Write the title and the child's name (author) on the cover page.
- Read through the book together.

Extensions/variations
- Make a collection of individual flap books.
- Make a larger flap book with the whole group, using two sheets of A3 and joining the two lots of flaps together after they are illustrated and the text is written.

Resources
- A4 sheet for each child
- Felt-tip pens
- Scissors
- Sticky tape

Communication, Language and Literacy

Feel free book

Making Books

• • • • • • • • •

Resources
- Paper
- Pens
- Crayons
- Pencils
- Scissors
- Coloured paper
- Sticky tape
- Hole punch
- String
- Staples

Learning objectives
- To use the vocabulary of books
- To link text words and illustrations
- To enjoy manipulating writing and drawing tools
- To give opportunities for expressing ideas and thoughts

Preparation
- Have a 'making books' table laid out with all of the book-making material. It will help if the children have made books with you before.

What to do
- Suggest to the children that they each make a book. Their book can be any kind of book they like, and they can make it about anything they want to make it about. Don't set any guidelines, let them treat the activity freely – as a kind of problem-solving exercise.
- As the children set about making their books, discuss the implications:
  - What do you want your book to look like?
  - How do you want to fix it together?
  - What do you want your book to be about?
  - Will it have pictures?
  - Will it have words?
  - Will you have to stick things in? What will you stick in?
  - Where will the pictures be?
  - Where will the words be?
  - Do you want to put numbers on the pages?
  - What will go on the cover?
- Encourage the children to do as much of the creative process as possible, including the 'writing', and get as much discussion and conversation going as you can. Remember to observe, wait and listen to give them the optimum opportunity for describing the task as they perform it.
- At the end of the creative process, get the children to 'read' and share their books with the others. Give lots of positive feedback.

Extensions/variations
- Make a display of all the books.
- Encourage individual children to share their books with other children and with other adults.

Links to home
- Encourage parents to make books with the children at home.

More flap books

Learning objectives
- To incorporate literacy into all areas of learning
- To show how pictures and texts link
- To compose captions and sentences

Preparation
- Make small books with the card or sugar paper by folding, stapling or tying it, whichever is the most appropriate. You don't need too many pages.

What to do
- Ask the child what she would like her book to be about and help her to find some appropriate pictures. You will need half as many pictures as you have pages.
- Help the child to glue her first chosen picture/photo on the first right-hand inside page. Talk about what she could write about it and help her to compose a caption or sentence. Use writing techniques appropriate to her level to help her write, or scribe the composed words.
- Invite the child to choose a piece of fabric or paper and cut it to cover the picture. Show the child how to glue it into place at the top of the picture, so that it provides a flap.
- Continue until all the pages are done.
- Help the child to make up the title for her flap book and do the front cover. Read through the book with the child, helping her to 'read' the words first and then looking under the flap to see the surprise. This will help her to understand the connection between words and pictures, and she will never tire of saying, 'I wonder what's under the flap…' even though she knows!

Extensions/variations
- Encourage the children to share their flap books with each other.
- Try to arrange a special sharing time with their parents, perhaps when they collect the children, when all the children and all the parents look at the books together.

Links to home
- Send books home for sharing.
- Encourage children and parents to make books at home and bring them in to share with the group.

Resources
- Card or sugar paper
- Scissors
- Felt-tip pens
- Glue-stick
- Photos or pictures cut from magazines or catalogues
- Scraps of different coloured and textured paper material or fabric, such as wallpaper, foil, shiny paper, lace, curtain fabric, etc

Communication, Language and Literacy

Wordless books

Any topic

Making Books

• • • • • • • • •

Resources
■ Card
■ Scissors
■ Colouring pens
■ Ring clips
■ Hole punch

Learning objectives
● To give opportunity to create a story
● To develop a good response to books

Preparation
● A book does not have to have *words* to make it work. Make up a book with a series of pictures and no text.

What to do
● Explain to the children that your book has pictures but no words. The pictures tell the story. Explain that you are not going to write the words of the story because everybody is going to be able to look at the pictures and remember it.
● Encourage the children to work out what the story should be. Each child does a picture of each event, colours it in and sticks it to the relevant page. When all the pictures are done, join the pages together and do the cover together.
● Get the children to go through the book and retell the story together.

Extensions/variations
● Look for wordless picture books in the local library.
● Encourage the children to read the pictures and tell the story to other children, adults, visitors and their parents.
● Make up the story by using a series of photographs linked to other themes or topics you are exploring in the group – eg you could show, in sequence, pictures of the children cooking or making something.

Related activity
● Right order (see page 96)

Print-a-book

Learning objective

● To use the computer for making a book

What to do

● First, create a story with the children. Make it simple, and include some of the concepts that the children are learning, such as colours, days of the week, numbers, etc. For example:

> *On Monday we do painting.*
> *On Tuesday we go for a walk.*
> *On Wednesday we play in the sand.*
> *On Thursday we make biscuits.*
> *On Friday we read some stories.*
> *On Saturday we stay in bed.*
> *On Sunday we get ready for*
> *tomorrow…*

● Use one page for each sentence. Choose a large font so that the children identify any letters they may be able to recognize.

● Type out a title page for the story, showing the children's names as authors.

● Print the story and secure the pages together. Get the children to illustrate the text by doing pictures on separate paper, cutting round them and sticking them to the pages with the words on.

Extensions/variations

● Make a book with several groups of children, using concepts they are learning about.

● Keep the books together in a display so that the children can share them with each other.

Links to home

● Encourage the children to take the books home to share with their families.

Resources

■ Computer
■ Word-processing program
■ Graphics program
■ Printer
■ Paper

Communication, Language and Literacy

© Irene Yates
www.brilliantpublications.co.uk

Simple pop-up books

Any topic

Resources

- Paper
- Pencils
- Felt-tip pens
- Scissors
- Glue-sticks
- Card

Learning objectives

- To develop awareness of characters in books
- To explore and experiment with words and texts

Preparation

- Fold each sheet of paper in half widthways. Turn down a small triangle from the fold and press it down, then straighten it up again and turn it down against the other side of the folded paper and press. Open the sheet of paper and push the triangle inside, then fold again and press.
- When you open the page, the triangle will pop up.

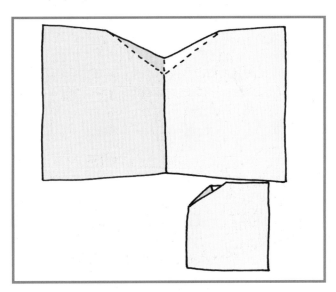

What to do

- Give the children a small piece of paper each to draw and colour a character on. Talk about who their character might be – is it someone they know, someone they have read about, someone they have made up?
- Fold the pictures down the centre so that the blank side of the paper is on the inside. Cut the characters out. If they are too small or complicated, cut an oval or rectangular shape around them.
- Carefully matching the folded lines, stick the characters on to the folded - down triangles so that the characters are *inside* the pages and, when you open the pages, they pop up.
- The children now need to compose some text about their page and their character, which you can scribe or help them to write using early or emergent writing strategies.
- Stick the pages back to back to make a book, and give it a cover.

Extension/variation

- It might be quite difficult, on the first attempt, to bring all of the characters into a consistent story line but, once the children have the idea of how the pop-up works, suggest you make up a story first together and then create the characters to fit it.

1–5

Zig-zag book

Learning objectives

- To give opportunities to incorporate literacy into all areas of learning
- To make a zig-zag book

Preparation

- Fold the pieces of card to make a zig-zag; the number of 'pages' will depend upon the length of your card.

What to do

- Discuss the concept of the book with the children. A zig-zag book can stand up along a shelf. It has pictures and/or text on both sides.

- Talk about what the book will be about – eg numbers, colours, pets, family, etc.
- Decide with the children which will be the first and, therefore, the title page – leave this until last.
- Cut, stick, write and draw the pictures and texts for the pages. Number the pages with the children, making sure they understand you don't number the title page (cover). When you get to the end of one side of the zig-zag, turn it over and carry on numbering.
- Decide on the title and demonstrate writing it and the authors' names.
- Read through the book together. Display it prominently.

Extensions/variations

- Help children to make individual books appropriate to their own lives and experiences.
- Encourage the children to use whatever writing techniques are appropriate for their stage of development.

Resources

- Card
- Felt-tip pens
- Glue
- Scissors
- Old magazines or catalogues

Book words

Making Books

• • • • • • • • •

Resources
- Lots of books
- A4 paper and card
- Ring clips
- Hole punch
- Pens
- Pencils

Learning objective
- To learn and use the vocabulary of books

Preparation
- Discuss the notion of making a book with the children. Decide together on a subject for the book, for example, our walk to the shops.

What to do
- Ask the children to tell you the various things that a book needs. You are aiming for them to use words such as:
  - Cover
  - Title
  - Author
  - Illustrator
  - Pages
  - Back
  - Front
  - Words
  - Letters
  - Pictures
  - Numbers (on pages).

- Decide how many pages your book will have. Add a front cover and a back cover. Secure the covers and pages.
- With each group do some pictures/illustrations and text/words for two pages, using book vocabulary all the time and encouraging the children to use it.
- When all the pages are finished, gather the groups together to decide on a title and how you will show who the author and illustrator. Demonstrate writing these.
- Number the pages.
- Go through the book with the children, asking questions that will elicit book vocabulary.

Extension/variation
- When using books with the children, use the vocabulary as a matter of course, showing the children that you expect them to use the words in future discussions.

Related activity
- Book know-how (see page 81)

Family album

Learning objectives
- To develop knowledge of books
- To know that print carries meaning
- To attempt writing for different purposes
- To know that information can be found in nonfiction texts

Preparation
- Make up a set of little books, one for each child. If you use three sheets of A4, folded, for each book, it will have 8 pages plus the inside of the front and back covers.

What to do
- Talk about families. Ask the children to suggest what a family is and who might belong to a family. Be sensitive towards children who feel they haven't got a family and explain, simply, that their family might be the people that they live with. Discuss the fact that there are all kinds of families and that is fine, we don't all have to be the same.
- Try to get the children to use relationship words – *mother, father, grandmother, grandfather, brother, sister, aunt, uncle, cousin.*
- Help the children to write *My Family* as their title, or *Who is this?* if they wish. Get them to write their name as author.

- Inside the book, ask the children to draw a picture on each page representing someone in their family and help them to write who it is –*my granddad, my nan, my cousin.* Encourage them to be as imaginative as possible – they might, for instance, put their favourite toy on the last page.

Extensions/variations
- Be sensitive to children with unconventional families. If there are difficulties, ask the children to make up a family, which needn't be 'real' – it could be an animal family or a toy family.
- Extend the writing by encouraging a sentence for each member of the family, eg *This is my dad cooking the dinner.*

Links to home
- Send the books home for the parents to share with the children.

Resources
- Paper
- Card
- Pencils
- Felt-tip pens
- Stapler

Making Books

• • • • • • • • • •

Resources

- Card
- Hole punch
- Felt-tip pens
- Paper
- Scissors
- Glue
- Sticky tape
- Pencils
- Crayons
- Ribbon or string
- *Rosie's Walk* by Pat Hutchins (Bodley Head)

Learning objective

- To create a story together, building upon the awareness of story structure

Preparation

- Talk to all the children about making a 'going for a walk' book before working with them individually. Make a simple book for each child, with three or four pages.

What to do

- Ask the child to do a small picture of herself on a piece of card and colour it in. Help her to cut it out. Stick one end of the string or ribbon to this cut-out with sticky tape.
- Make up the story of the walk. It might be a walk to the park or the shops. Invite the child to make up a sentence for each page and scribe it for her, demonstrating how you write the letters and pointing out the words as you go. Help her to illustrate each page.
- Do the cover together, working out the title and writing the child's name as author.
- Make a small pocket with card and tape it to the front cover. Tape the other end of the string or ribbon into this pocket and then place the cut-out child into the pocket.
- When she opens her book to read the story, the child slips the cut-out of herself out of the pocket and 'walks' it along with the story.

Extensions/variations

- If the children are able, let them make the books themselves, using A4 sheets as pages and just help them to put them together.
- Read *Rosie's Walk* with the children.
- Make a 'going for a walk' book of it.
- Keep all of the books easily accessible for reading and sharing.

(1)

Joshua's Walk

Communication, Language and Literacy

I-spy alphabet book

Making Books

• • • • • • • • •

Learning objectives
- To identify sounds and letters
- To incorporate literacy into other areas of learning
- To show how pictures and texts link
- To familiarize children with alphabetical order

Preparation
- Make sure that the children are familiar with and able to play the game 'I-Spy'.
- On 26 sheets, write the words, *I spy with my little eye, something beginning with…*

What to do
- You will need the 26 pages and a page for the front cover of the book, though you might choose to do, say, three or four letters only in each session.
- On each page, with the children, read the words 'I spy…' and go through the alphabet (use a visual aid if you have one on display). Say the words together, then you write the letter. If you have introduced capitals, say the name and the sound, and write both. As you are writing, ask the children to trace the letters in the air, and ask them where you will start the letter.

- Take suggestions from the children for things they can see beginning with the relevant letter in:
  - the group's base
  - their home
  - the park
  - the shops
  and write them on the appropriate page.
- At the end of the session, go through the letters you have covered and the things the children have identified.

Extensions/variations
- Ask the children to draw or cut out pictures to stick into the alphabet book.
- Reinforce the notion of alphabetical order by going through the pages.

Resources
- Sugar paper
- Ring clips or treasury tags
- Paper to draw on
- Scissors
- Glue
- Felt-tip pens

Communication, Language and Literacy

www.brilliantpublications.co.uk

Jigsaw template

Rhyming pairs template

Communication, Language and Literacy

Letter train template

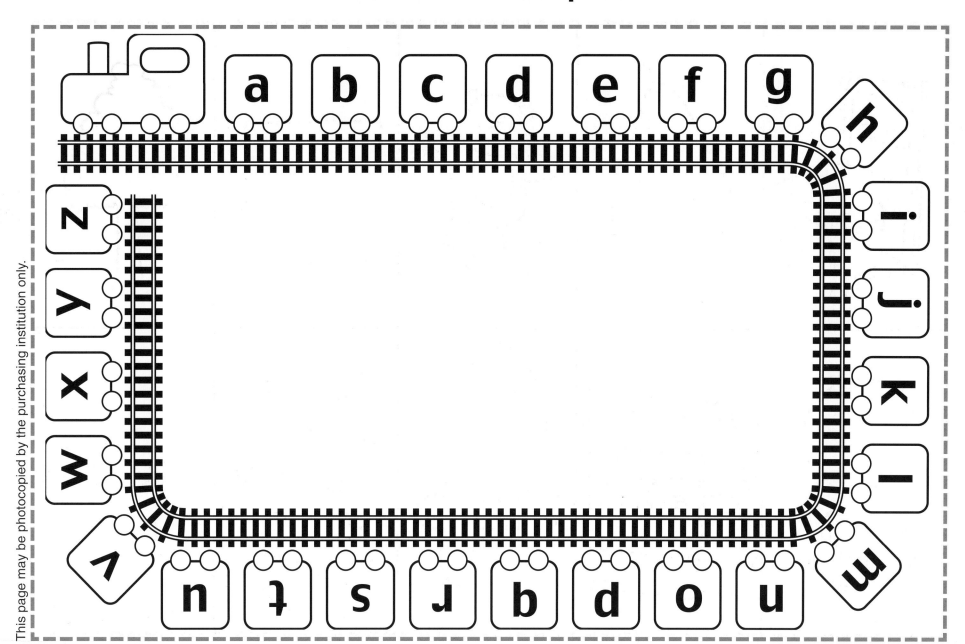

Same and different template

Communication, Language and Literacy

Order, order template

Match the letter template, 1

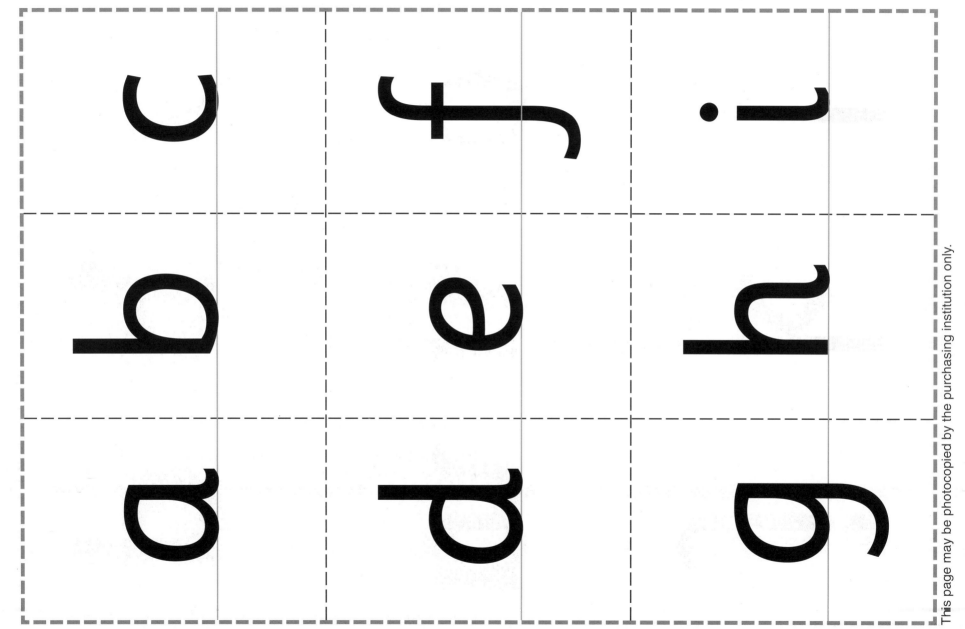

Communication, Language and Literacy

© Irene Yates
www.brilliantpublications.co.uk

Match the letter template, 2

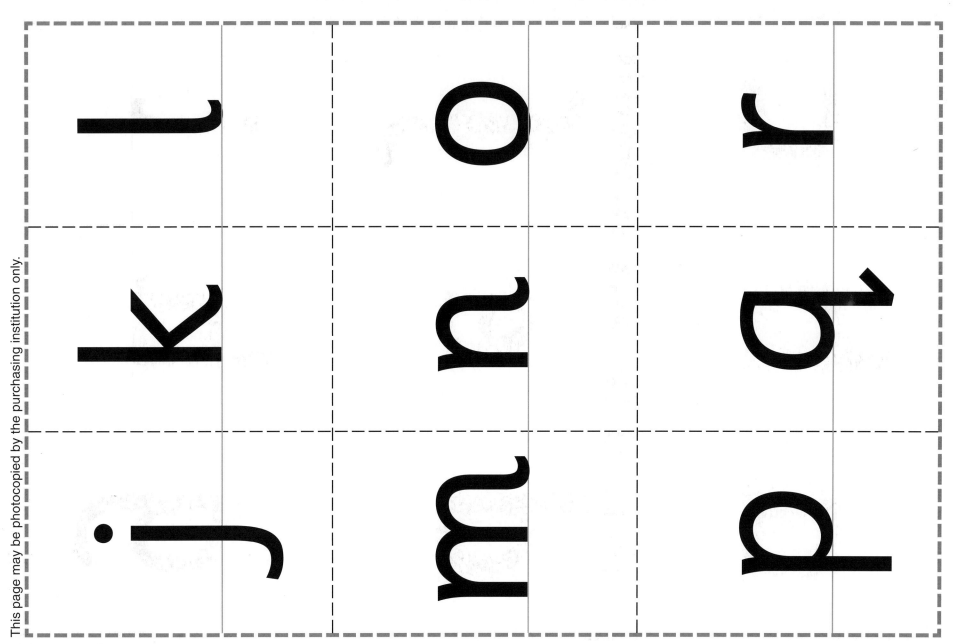

© Irene Yates
www.brilliantpublications.co.uk

Match the letter template, 3

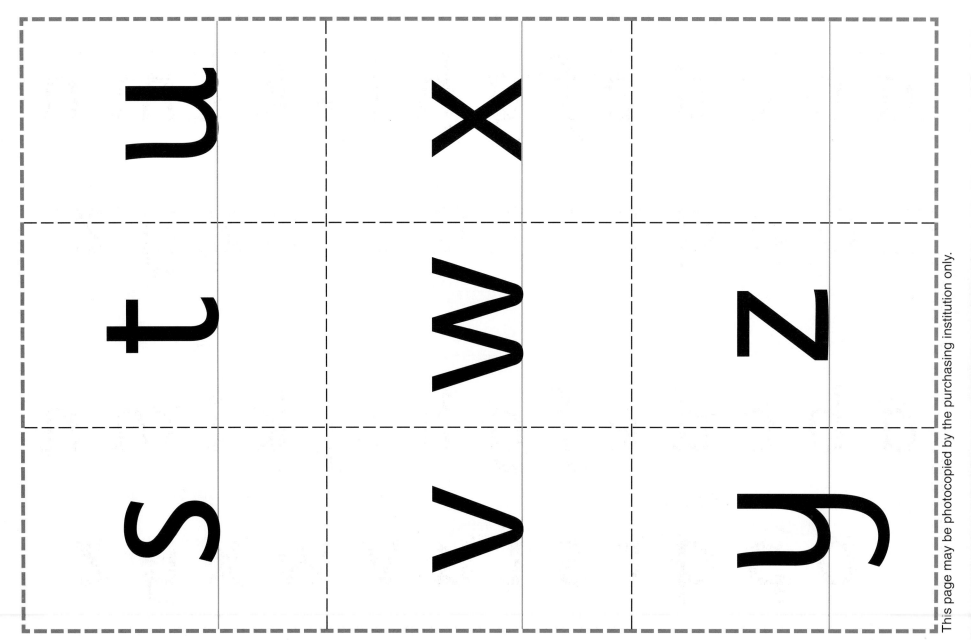

Communication, Language and Literacy

© Irene Yates
www.brilliantpublications.co.uk

Forming letters

a b c d e f g h i j k l m n

o p q r s t u v w x y z

a b c d e f g h i j k l m n

o p q r s t u v w x y z

Rhymes

Action rhymes

Here is the church

Here is the church	(*touch fists at knuckles*)
And here is the steeple,	(*open fists and touch fingertips*)
Open the doors	(*open hands wide*)
And see all the people.	(*wriggle fingers*)

Here is the vicar going upstairs
(*walk fingers upwards*)
And here he is, a-saying his prayers.
(*hands together for prayer*)

Incy Wincy spider

Incy Wincy spider	
Climbing up the spout.	(*fingers climbing into air*)
Down comes the rain	
To wash the spider out.	(*flutter fingers down*)
Out comes the sunshine	
To dry up all the rain,	(*stretch hands out for sunshine*)

Incy Wincy spider climbing up again!
(*fingers climb high into air*)

I hear thunder, I hear thunder

I hear thunder, I hear thunder,
Hark, don't you? Hark, don't you?
(*hands to ears, listening*)
Pitter patter raindrops, pitter patter raindrops,
(*hands fluttering down as rain*)
I'm wet through! So are you!

Two little dickie birds

Two little dickie birds	
Sitting on a wall	(*make beak shapes with each hand, by putting thumb and forefinger together*)
One named Peter, one named Paul.	
	(*open each beak in turn*)
Fly away, Peter! Fly away, Paul!	
	(*flutter each hand behind back*)
Come back, Peter! Come back, Paul!	
	(*flutter each hand back*)

Communication, Language and Literacy

The wheels on the bus go round and round

The wheels on the bus go round and round,
(*hands rolling round each other*)
Round and round, round and round,
(*repeat movement*)
The wheels on the bus go round and round,
(*repeat movement*)

All day long.

The driver on the bus goes, 'Sit down, please,
(*wagging finger*)
Sit down, please, sit down, please'
(*repeat movement*)
The driver on the bus goes, 'Sit down, please,'
(*repeat movement*)

All day long.

The old men on the bus go nod, nod, nod,
(*nodding, tiredness*)
Nod, nod, nod, nod, nod, nod,
(*repeat movement*)
The old men on the bus go nod, nod, nod,
(*repeat movement*)

All day long.

The ladies on the bus go chitter, chatter, chitter, (*chattering movements*)
Chitter, chatter, chitter, chitter, chatter, chitter, (*repeat movement*)
The ladies on the bus go chitter, chatter, chitter, (*repeat movement*)

All day long.

The horn on the bus goes honk, honk, honk,
(*thumb and fingers together*)
Honk, honk, honk, honk, honk, honk,
(*repeat movement*)
The horn on the bus goes honk, honk, honk,
(*repeat movement*)

All day long.

The babies on the bus go wah, wah, wah,
(*exaggerated crying expressions*)
Wah, wah, wah, wah, wah, wah,
(*repeat movement*)
The babies on the bus go wah, wah, wah,
(*repeat movement*)

All day long.

Tommy Thumb

Tommy Thumb, Tommy Thumb, where are you?
Here I am, here I am,   (*wriggle thumbs*)
How do you do?
Peter Pointer, Peter Pointer, where are you?
Here I am, here I am,   (*wriggle first fingers*)
How do you do?
Middleman Tall, Middleman Tall, where are you?
Here I am, here I am,   (*wriggle middle fingers*)
How do you do?
Ruby Ring, Ruby Ring, where are you?
Here I am, here I am,   (*wriggle third fingers*)
How do you do?
Baby Small, Baby Small, where are you?
Here I am, here I am,   (*put up little fingers*)
How do you do?

Marching rhyme

The grand old Duke of York

The grand old Duke of York
He had ten thousand men,
He marched them up to the top of the hill
And he marched them down again.
And when they were up, they were up.
And when they were down, they were down.
And when they were only halfway up
They were neither up nor down!

Clapping rhymes

Rain, rain, go away

Rain, rain, go away,
Come again another day.
Rain, rain, go away,
Come again another day.

Pat-a-cake, pat-a-cake

Pat-a-cake, pat-a-cake,
Baker's man,
Bake me a cake as fast as you can.
Pit it and pat it and mark it with (*child's initial*),
Put it in the oven for (*child's name*) and me!

Hot cross buns!

Hot cross buns! Hot cross buns!
One a penny, two a penny, hot cross buns!
If you have no daughters, give them to your sons,
One a penny, two a penny, hot cross buns!

© Irene Yates
www.brilliantpublications.co.uk

If you're happy and you know it

If you're happy and you know it, clap your hands,
            (*clap, clap*)
If you're happy and you know it, clap your hands,
            (*clap, clap*)
If you're happy and you know it, and you really want to show it,
If you're happy and you know it, clap your hands.
            (*clap, clap*)

(*Substitute other actions and sounds, eg 'nod your head', 'say boo', etc.*)

Rhymes to learn and recite

Little Boy Blue
Little Boy Blue
Come blow your horn,
The sheep's in the meadow,
The cow's in the corn.
Where is the boy
Who looks after the sheep?
He's under a haystack
Fast asleep.
Will you wake him?
No, not I,
For if I do
He's sure to cry.

Three blind mice
Three blind mice,
Three blind mice,
See how they run!
See how they run!
They all ran after the farmer's wife,
Who cut off their tails with a carving knife,
Did you ever see such a thing in your life
As three blind mice?

See-saw, Margery Daw
See-saw, Margery Daw,
Johnny will have a new master.
He shall pay but a penny a day,
because he can't work any faster.

One, two, buckle my shoe
One, two, buckle my shoe;
Three, four, knock at the door;
Five, six, pick up sticks;
Seven, eight, lay them straight;
Nine, ten, my fat hen,
Eleven, twelve, dig and delve;
Thirteen, fourteen, maids a-courting;
Fifteen, sixteen, maids in the kitchen,
Seventeen, eighteen, maids in waiting;
Nineteen, twenty, my plate's empty.

There was a crooked man
There was a crooked man
And he walked a crooked mile,
He found a crooked sixpence
Upon a crooked stile;
He bought a crooked cat,
Which caught a crooked mouse,
And they all lived together
In a little crooked house.

Hickory, dickory, dock
Hickory, dickory, dock,
The mouse ran up the clock,
The clock struck one,
The mouse ran down,
Hickory, dickory, dock.

One, two, three, four, five
One, two, three, four, five,
Once I caught a fish alive,
Six, seven, eight, nine, ten,
Then I let it go again.
Why did you let it go?
Because it bit my finger so.
Which finger did it bite?
This little finger on the right.

Peter Piper picked a peck
Peter Piper picked a peck
Of pickled pepper;
A peck of pickled pepper
Peter Piper picked.
If Peter Piper picked a peck
Of pickled pepper,
Where's the peck of pickled pepper
Peter Piper picked?

She sells sea-shells
She sells sea-shells
On the sea shore;
The shells she sells
Are sea-sells, I'm sure.
So if she sells sea-shells
On the sea shore,
I'm sure that the shells
Are sea shore shells.

If all the world were paper
If all the world were paper,
If all the sea were ink,
If all the trees were bread and cheese,
What should we have to drink?

Communication, Language and Literacy

© Irene Yates
www.brilliantpublications.co.uk

Doctor Foster went to Gloucester

Doctor Foster went to Gloucester
In a shower of rain;
He stepped in a puddle,
Right up to his middle,
And never went there again.

Tom, Tom, the piper's son

Tom, Tom, the piper's son,
Stole a pig and away he run:
The pig was eat, and Tom was beat,
And Tom went howling down the street.

Ride a cock-horse to Banbury Cross

Ride a cock-horse to Banbury Cross
To see a fine lady upon a white horse;
With rings on her fingers and bells on her toes
She shall have music wherever she goes.

Pussy-cat, pussy-cat

Pussy-cat, pussy-cat,
Where have you been?
I've been to London to visit the queen.
Pussy-cat, pussy-cat,
What did you there?
I frightened a little mouse under her chair!

Little Miss Muffet

Little Miss Muffet, sat on a tuffet,
Eating her curds and whey,
Along came a spider
Who sat down beside her
And frightened Miss Muffet away.

I hear thunder

I hear thunder,
I hear thunder,
Hark! Don't you?
Hark, don't you?
Pitter patter raindrops,
Pitter patter raindrops,
I'm wet through.
So are you!

Here we go round the mulberry bush

Here we go round the mulberry bush, the mulberry bush,
    the mulberry bush;
Here we go round the mulberry bush, on a cold and frosty
    morning.

This is the way we…

(*wash our hands, clean our teeth, march up and down, reach the sky, etc*)

Twinkle, twinkle, little star
Twinkle, twinkle, little star,
How I wonder what you are,
Up above the world so high,
Like a diamond in the sky.

Hey diddle, diddle
Hey diddle, diddle,
The cat and the fiddle,
The cow jumped over the moon.
The little dog laughed
To see such fun
And the dish ran away with the spoon.

Diddle, diddle, dumpling
Diddle, diddle, dumpling,
My son John
Went to bed with his trousers on.
One stocking off and one stocking on,
Diddle, diddle, dumpling,
My son John.

Half a pound of tuppenny rice
Half a pound of tuppenny rice,
Half a pound of treacle,
Mix it up and make it nice,
Pop goes the weasel!
Up and down the City Road,
In and out the Eagle,
That's the way the money goes,
Pop goes the weasel!

It's raining, it's pouring
It's raining, it's pouring,
The old man is snoring,
He went to bed
And bumped his head
And couldn't get up in the morning!

© Irene Yates
www.brilliantpublications.co.uk

Story lines

Goldilocks and the Three Bears

One day, Goldilocks was walking through the woods when she came to a little cottage. She opened the door and went in. In the kitchen were three bowls of porridge on the table.

Goldilocks tried the porridge in the biggest bowl. It was much too hot.

She tried the porridge in the middle-sized bowl. It was much too cold.

She tried the porridge in the smallest bowl. It was just right, so she ate it all up.

There were three chairs in the living room.

Goldilocks tried the biggest chair. It was much too hard.

She tried the middle-sized chair. It was much too soft.

She tried the smallest chair. It was just right, so she sat herself in it. But she was much too heavy and the chair broke into little pieces.

Goldilocks went upstairs. There were three beds in the bedroom.

She tried the biggest bed. It was much too high.

She tried the middle-sized bed. It was much too low.

She tried the smallest bed. It was just right, so she went fast asleep.

The three bears who lived in the cottage came home. They saw at once that something was wrong.

'Who's been eating my porridge?' growled Father Bear.
'Who's been eating my porridge?' growled Mother Bear.
'Who's been eating my porridge?' squeaked Baby Bear, 'And they've eaten it all up!'

They went into the living room.

'Who's been sitting in my chair?' growled Father Bear.
'Who's been sitting in my chair?' growled Mother Bear.
'Who's been sitting in my chair?' squeaked Baby Bear, 'And they've broken it all up!'

They went up to the bedroom.

'Who's been sleeping in my bed?' growled Father Bear.
'Who's been sleeping in my bed?' growled Mother Bear.
'Who's been sleeping in my bed?' squeaked Baby Bear, 'And she's still there!'

Then Goldilocks woke up and ran down the stairs and out of the door and off through the woods before the three bears could catch her!

Rumpelstiltskin

Once upon a time there was a very silly man who had a beautiful daughter.

The father said, 'She's not just beautiful. She is so clever she can spin straw into gold.'

The King heard about the beautiful, clever daughter and had her brought to the palace.

He said, 'If she spins this straw into gold, I will marry her. But if she doesn't, she will die.'

The beautiful daughter was put into a turret with a pile of straw. She burst into tears. How could she spin gold out of straw?

Suddenly a little man appeared. 'Give me your gold ring,' he said, 'and I will spin the straw into gold for you.'

The next day the King was so pleased about the gold, he decided he wanted some more. 'You have to do it again tonight,' he said to the beautiful daughter, 'to prove it wasn't a trick.'

When the daughter cried again, the little man appeared. 'I'll spin the straw into gold,' he said, 'if you give me your beautiful necklace.' So she did.

Of course, the greedy King wanted more gold, so that night the beautiful daughter was shut up in a room full of straw.

She cried and cried and cried. The little man appeared. But the beautiful daughter had nothing left to give him.

'That's all right,' said the little man, 'when you are Queen I will have your first baby for my own.'

The beautiful daughter was so frightened, she agreed. The next morning, there was so much gold, the King said, 'Start the wedding celebrations right away!' and the beautiful daughter became his Queen.

After a year, the Queen had a lovely baby girl of her own. She'd forgotten all about the little man, but one night he appeared. 'I've come to collect the baby,' he said, 'just as you promised.'

'No,' cried the Queen. 'I'll give you anything you want, but not my baby!'

The little man laughed. 'If you can guess my name before three nights have passed, I won't take your baby. But if you can't – the baby will be mine!'

On the next two nights, the Queen guessed every name she could think of but none of them was the name of the little man.

On the third day, one of the King's soldiers came to the Queen. He said, 'I saw a funny little man in the woods. He was dancing and singing. He sang, *The Queen will never win my game, for Rumpelstiltskin is my name!*'

When the little man came that night, the Queen said, 'Is your name Hurly Burly?'

'No,' chuckled the little man.

'Is it Humpelby Bumpelby?'

'No,' chuckled the little man, rubbing his hands together gleefully.

'Is it – Rumpelstiltskin?' asked the Queen.

The little man turned red with anger and he stamped his feet so hard that he fell right through the floor of the palace.
And the Queen lived happily ever after.

The Three Billy Goats Gruff

Three billy goats gruff lived in a field. They wanted to cross to the other side, to eat the best grass. But a troll lived under the bridge and if they crossed they knew he would try to eat them up.

The smallest billy goat gruff was first to cross the bridge. Trip, trap, trip, trap. The troll jumped up and said, 'Who's that crossing my bridge? I'm going to eat you up!'

The smallest billy goat said, 'Please don't eat me. My brother is bigger then me and he's coming next.' So the troll let him pass.

The middle-sized billy goat gruff was next to cross the bridge. Trip, trap, trip, trap. The troll jumped up and said, 'Who's that crossing my bridge? I'm going to eat you up!'

The middle-sized billy goat said, 'Please don't eat me. My brother is bigger then me and he's coming next.' So the troll let him pass.

Then it was the big billy goat gruff's turn to cross the bridge. Trip, trap, trip, trap. The troll jumped up and said, 'Who's that crossing my bridge? I'm going to eat you up!'

'Oh, no you're not!' cried the big billy goat and he put down his horns and tossed the troll into the air.

The troll fell into the river with a splash and the three billy goats gruff happily munched away on the other side of the river.

The Three Little Pigs

Once upon a time there were three little pigs who set off into the wide world together.

They met a farmer carrying a bale of straw. The first pig said, 'I could build a house with that.' So he bought the straw and started to build a house.

The other two pigs went on. They met a woodcutter carrying a bundle of sticks. The second pig said, 'I could build a house with those.' So he bought the sticks and started to build a house.

The third pig went on. He met a workman pushing a barrow full of bricks. He said, 'I could build a house with those.' So he bought the bricks and started to build a house.

One night, the first pig was asleep in his house of straw, when a wolf came by.
'Little pig, little pig, let me in,' called the wolf.
'No, no, no, by the hair on my chinny, chin, chin, I will not let you in!' cried the pig.

'Then I'll huff and I'll puff and I'll blow your house down!' cried the wolf. And he did.

The first little pig ran to the second little pig's house of sticks. The next night the two pigs were asleep in the house of sticks, when the wolf came by. 'Little pigs, little pigs, let me in,' called the wolf.

'No, no, no, by the hair on my chinny, chin, chin, I will not let you in!' cried the pigs.

'Then I'll huff and I'll puff and I'll blow your house down!' cried the wolf. And he did.

The little pigs ran to the third little pig's house of bricks. The next night the three pigs were asleep in the house of bricks, when the wolf came by. 'Little pigs, little pigs, let me in,' called the wolf.

'No, no, no, by the hair on my chinny, chin, chin, I will not let you in!' cried the pigs.

'Then I'll huff and I'll puff and I'll blow your house down!' cried the wolf. And he huffed and he puffed but he could not blow the house down.

The wolf was so angry, he said, 'If you don't let me in, I'm going to climb down the chimney!'

But the third little pig was much cleverer than the wolf. Quickly he put a pot water on to the fire and when the wolf came down the chimney, splash! he went into the pot, and that was the end of him!

The Gingerbread man
Once upon a time there lived a little old man and a little old woman, in the country. One day the little old lady had some gingerbread mixture left over.

'I'll make a little gingerbread man,' she said to herself. She cut out the shape of a gingerbread man. She made him eyes and three buttons out of raisins. Then she popped him in the oven to bake.

The old woman heard a sound coming from the oven. She opened the door slowly. The little gingerbread man jumped up from the oven and ran out through the kitchen door. 'Come back!' shouted the old woman.

Her husband began to run after her and the gingerbread man. 'Come back,' he shouted.

But the gingerbread man called over his shoulder, 'Run, run, as fast as you can. You can't catch me, I'm the gingerbread man!'

© Irene Yates
www.brilliantpublications.co.uk

He ran out of the gate and past a cow who was chewing grass. 'Come back!' cried the cow, and she joined in the chase.

But the gingerbread man kept on running. 'The little old woman and the little old man couldn't catch me. And neither will you! Run, run, as fast as you can. You can't catch me, I'm the gingerbread man!'

In the next field was a horse, eating hay.
'Come back!' cried the horse, and he joined in the chase.

But the gingerbread man kept on running. 'The little old woman and the little old man and the cow couldn't catch me. And neither will you! Run, run, as fast as you can. You can't catch me, I'm the gingerbread man!'

On the gate, perched a rooster, eating grain.
'Come back!' cried the rooster, and he joined in the chase.

But the gingerbread man kept on running. 'The little old woman and the little old man and the cow and the horse couldn't catch me. And neither will you! Run, run, as fast as you can. You can't catch me, I'm the gingerbread man!'

In the yard, was a pig, eating slop.
'Come back!' cried the pig, and he joined in the chase.

But the gingerbread man kept on running. 'The little old woman and the little old man and the cow and the horse and the rooster couldn't catch me. And neither will you! Run, run, as fast as you can. You can't catch me, I'm the gingerbread man!'

At the end of the next field, the gingerbread man came to a wide river. He had to stop because, although he could run, he didn't know how to swim.

A big, red fox sat nearby. 'Can I help you?' said the fox. 'Just jump on my back and I'll take you across the river.'

So the gingerbread man jumped on to the fox's back. The fox slid into the river and began to swim across.

'The water is getting deeper,' said the fox. 'Climb on my head to keep yourself dry.'

So the gingerbread man did, and the fox swam on.

'The water is getting even deeper,' said the fox. 'Climb on to my nose to keep yourself dry.'

But as soon as the gingerbread man climbed on to the fox's nose, the fox threw up his head and the gingerbread man flew up into the air. Then down he fell, right into the fox's mouth. 'Snap! Snap!' went the fox.

And the gingerbread man was gone.

Topic index

© Irene Yates
www.brilliantpublications.co.uk